D0458102

A Day in Part 15

A Day in Part 15

Law & Order
in Family Court

By Judge Richard Ross

Four Walls Eight Windows
New York / London

Published in the United States by
Four Walls Eight Windows
39 West 14th Street
New York, NY, 10011

U.K. offices:
Four Walls Eight Windows/Turnaround
Unit 3, Olympia Trading Estate
Coburg Road, Wood Green
London N22 6TZ

First printing March 1997

Library of Congress Cataloging-in-Publication Data:
Ross, Richard, 1944-
A day in part 15 : law & order in family court / by Richard Ross.
   p. cm:
ISBN 1-56858-089-4
1. New York (State). Family Court (City of New York) 2. Juvenile courts—New York (State)—New York. 3. Juvenile justice, Administration of—New York (State)—New York. I. Title.
KFN5116.5.Z9R67 1997
346.74701'5'0269—dc21   96-40292
                                                                      CIP

10 9 8 7 6 5 4 3 2 1

Book design by Acme Art, Inc.
Printed in the United States

To Laura

AUTHOR'S NOTE

All names herein are fictitious. Many of the case descriptions are representative, not actual. With the exception of one case, in which my published opinion has the title *Anonymous* v. *Anonymous*, facts were changed to assure anonymity in all instances where real cases informed the narrative. Courtrooms are called "parts" in the New York City Family Court; there is no Part 15 in the Bronx Family Court.

Many thanks to JillEllyn Riley, senior editor at Four Walls Eight Windows, the compleat professional this novice needed; Carl DeSantis for sound advice as well as helpful direction with an early draft; Hon. Rhoda Cohen and Ilana Gruebel for savvy critiques; Ilana for research, too; Karen Golightly and Dennis M. Dreyfus for great eyes and good ideas; Clare McHugh for polish and practicality; and Mark Lasswell for believing in the manuscript and giving it wings.

A Day in Part 15

INTRODUCTION

I took the judicial oath from the mayor and started packing my office. The phone rang.

"Congratulations, Rick," said a judge of thirty years. "And don't worry, there's life after Family Court."

"What do you mean?"

He laughed. "Just make sure you go to bed early."

On that August morning in 1991, I was forty-seven years old. Years ago I had left the courtroom for a career in court administration. I liked the work and valued my contribution. Yet I was still searching for the main chance; the crown of a courts career was a judgeship. And the Family Court appointment lasted ten years, with a nice pay raise besides. My career path hadn't exactly merged with the road to riches, and my wife Laura and I had our son Luke on the way.

I felt lucky as well, at last having managed the final connection to the appointment. The year-long nominating process was arduous and nerve-racking, consisting of three lengthy questionnaires and four interviews with various committees and subcommittees before I even met the mayor. My performance didn't embarrass my sponsors, and certainly my hard work over the years had made a good impression. Yet, many others I met

along the road also had sound backing and presented themselves well, but failed to make the final cut.

Such were my thoughts on induction day at city hall. The
power of the law, the responsibility of judging, the exhaustion
and isolation to come, the pride the work could bring—all of
these were as yet unimagined.

Uneasiness set in the day after induction, a Friday. First,
word that there is "life after Family Court." Then, just a few
minutes later, a call from another judge.

"Don't panic," she said.

"I'm not."

"Good."

A pause. Then: "Should I?"

"Well, you've been away from the courtroom for a little
while. Better start reading some law. Tactics you'll pick up later."

Tactics?

The Family Court's administrative judge called. We went
back twenty years. I took a casual approach.

"So," I said to her, "it looks as though you're going to have
me to kick around a while longer. Any chance of my being
assigned to Manhattan?"

I'd been working downtown for a long time and was living
on Manhattan's Upper East Side. Would I be able to handle the
adjustment of assignment to Brooklyn, Queens, the Bronx, or
Staten Island—New York City's so-called outer boroughs? I
gave a cute laugh, but my heart was going rat-a-tat.

"You must be kidding," she said. "You're going to the
Bronx. Actually, by the caseload numbers you ought to be going
to Brooklyn, but we don't have a courtroom for you there.

You're the new kid on the block. You want Manhattan, you have to get in line."

The Bronx! A rush hollowed my stomach. I was born in Brooklyn, raised in Queens, and as an adult lived on Staten Island and in Manhattan. Drive me in a car and remove my blindfold anywhere in those four boroughs, I'd have my bearings in a moment. But the Bronx! I could find any seat in Yankee Stadium in my sleep, the rest was unfamiliar turf.

A week would pass before I reported there, a period filled with calls from well-wishers, ego-boosting conversations with family and friends, dozens of cards in the mail offering congratulations, and farewell parties at work. I received traditional gifts, including a judicial dress robe (for taking formal pictures and performing weddings) and a plainer, lightweight robe for daily use on the bench. Among the gifts were two gavels. One was a standard wooden gavel. The other, from my staff, was made of foam rubber attached to the cardboard cylinder of a toilet paper roll—it would reflect the quality and force of my rulings, they told me.

And people started calling me "Judge." It seemed artificial to me. I responded with an awkward grin or self-conscious chuckle.

Heady stuff. I was leaving the world of work as I had known it, a world of lawyers and bureaucrats, of politicians and technicians and meetings and gossip and rumors and power plays, of lunches and committees and reports, a social life and culture whose currency was information, affect, and relationships, the nervous incestuous hive of government. Ahead of me was . . . what, exactly? The inside of a courtroom: that for sure. But what else?

"Forget about that other world," still another Family Court judge told me. "It's gone. Your circle is going to shrink. You'll have your wife, your closest personal friends, and the other judges, at least the few you'll have the time to talk to."

I studied law most of the first weekend, bringing myself up-to-date with recent caselaw and breaking for Sunday brunch on the West Side with a friend, a Family Court judge I'd come to know well during my years in bureaucracy. We talked about the basic Family Court case types: domestic violence, child custody and visitation, child neglect and abuse, paternity, termination of parental rights, adoption, and juvenile delinquency, which was actually the broad field of criminal law and procedure as applied to children under sixteen. Once upon a time I had practiced law in Family Court, in New York and elsewhere. Much of what we discussed was familiar to me, but my friend gave caution.

"Your old experience will be a plus, but times have changed. The cases are harder than they used to be, and there are lots more of them, around 220,000 last year and only forty-seven judges. When you were practicing, not that many teenagers dealt drugs. You didn't see twelve-year-olds carrying guns. Crack didn't exist and there were fewer parents on heroin. The volume of domestic violence cases is frightening. Three times as many kids are in foster care than when you practiced. There's more sex abuse. More unpaid child support. Mentally ill people out on the streets, some with their children. Even relatively stable families can't always find adequate housing. More and more kids can't read. And it's not just the poor. People with money come to court with drug and alcohol problems, and middle-class spouses and kids get abused, too."

He continued, "More than a few of these cases give us no selection; sometimes there's just no good choice. You'll see, family law guidelines are still relatively broad, not much different than when you were in the court. Mostly we're judging people's credibility all day and applying basic good human values within the legal standards."

Over coffee he gave me pointers on some of the types of hearings. These range from brief proceedings for temporary orders of protection in domestic violence cases to hearings over whether to remove a child from a parent's home for child neglect to full-blown child custody trials. Ordinary and special rules of evidence applied. There are no juries in the New York City Family Court; the judge is both fact finder and arbiter of the law. This, my friend told me, took a special kind of concentration and facility. There would be a large daily calendar to manage that on a typical day would average fifty to sixty cases. In the courtroom would be two court officers, my law assistant, a clerk, and a court stenographer, all of whom would know not only their own jobs, of course, but to some extent mine, better than I would for a time.

I sensed the pride my friend felt in being a Family Court judge. Though he didn't so much as say it, he seemed to be telling me that Family Court judges were a special breed of hard-working, facile magicians who combined the wisdom of Solomon with legal genius and the instincts of street fighters.

"The main thing is to use your common sense and trust your gut. Don't be afraid to make decisions or you'll die up there. And try not to reserve decision except in special cases. Rule from the bench. You can't work nights and weekends in this job. You'll burn out, there are too many cases. Once in a while on an especially interesting case you can reserve decision and write an opinion if you want. Whatever you do, don't take the job home with you. Just wipe it from your mind at the end of the day."

I gulped. He must have noticed.

"You'll be fine, I can tell," he told me, he of the twelve years of experience and deep well of confidence. I wondered.

Now I was sent on a week-long tour of courtrooms in Queens, Manhattan, and Brooklyn, during which I sat at the bench, sans robe, at the side of the judge presiding. I hated it, feeling self-conscious and full of nerves, like a rookie sent to the majors before his time. Introduced all day to court staff and lawyers, I couldn't think of a thing to say after thanking them for their congratulations on my appointment. Quickly it became apparent that conversation wasn't their intent. And to me it seemed inappropriate, even improper, to be too familiar with them. Such a strange understanding and turn of events, after years of commerce in a world in which the force of personality and the quality of relationships were the principal forms of currency.

On Monday I was to report to Queens Family Court. A court security officer would be waiting for me in the court's parking lot and would escort me from my car to the courtroom of the supervising judge. Would be waiting for me. (Imagine that.) Would escort me. (How strange.) As I drove into the parking lot, I had the full sense of entering the unknown. I felt less the fluttering of butterflies than the jolt of a tectonic event.

Yes, a uniformed court officer did meet me in the parking lot that morning and escort me to the courtroom and call me "Judge" half a dozen times. And he was highly professional in demeanor and action, a quality of job performance that the court officers would demonstrate routinely to me over time. I spent the next hour observing one of my new colleagues in action, a man with nine years of judicial experience who whisked through the calendar. I noticed how quick he was to become excited, how his body and tone filled with aggression when a lawyer or litigant tried to move the judge's script to the margins and how quickly he moved it back to center page.

"He has an awfully quick trigger," I remarked to my Family Court judge friend.

"He's a really good judge, Rick," my friend replied, looking serious. "Very practical, lots of common sense, very fast. He might be a little hot for your taste, but he doesn't demean anybody. Everyone's got their own style."

"What about due process?"

His look was withering. "You don't know enough even to raise the issue yet. You'll discover your own quirks soon enough, Mr. Justice Brandeis."

The next day I watched another Queens judge do her calendar. She'd been on the bench for seven years. Her style was without fireworks, and she seemed to me marvelously on target as far as the issues and the scores of people with whom she dealt all day. And efficient!

"You sure did a number on that calendar," I told her.

Courtroom staff were putting the furniture in place and finishing the day's paperwork. The court stenographer packed his machine. The courtroom had the air of a theater winding down after performance.

"Nah," the judge said. "Just another quiet summer day in Queens."

"Quiet? You did forty-eight cases."

"It really wasn't much. A nice break."

I thought she had worked her head off.

"Well, I'm impressed, at least," I said.

"Thanks," she said, seeming distracted.

Observing other judges had a quickly diminishing return for me as a training technique. Underlying whatever else I was thinking or feeling was anxiety, plain and simple. How well would I handle the situation I had just observed? How was it possible for me to learn everything I apparently needed to know? How good were my instincts? My head was starting to spin.

One afternoon I sat with a judge and watched a performance of such dignity, command of the courtroom, and legal precision that I despaired of my own possibilities.

"God, what an ego problem, you're so competitive," my judge friend said when I relayed my impression. "You're right, she's excellent. But I would bore myself to death with her style."

Then, on Friday of that week, I spent two hours in court with a Brooklyn judge of sixteen-years experience. He breezed through his calendar with efficiency and competence, keeping, I felt, great distance from the lawyers and public but maintaining a hilariously irreverent side conversation with me, the court clerk, and the court officers that was inaudible to everyone else in his large, acoustically deficient courtroom.

Halfway through the afternoon, unexpectedly, the judge said to me, "Time for you to put on the robe and do a couple."

Gulp.

"I didn't bring my robe." That ought to end that.

He stood up. "Here, you can wear mine."

The court officers, court stenographer, and clerk were grinning. They'd seen this before, of course, but it was always interesting and broke up their otherwise routine plow through the calendar.

I stood. "Here, turn around," the judge said.

Standing, I removed my suit jacket and put my arms out behind me to slip into his robe. Immediately, my left arm became stuck halfway down the sleeve.

"Uh, it's not going in," I said to him.

"There's a tear in there," the judge said. "Take your arm out."

I felt like a boy at a shoelace-tying lesson.

I tried again. Again, stuck.

"I don't know, Judge," the clerk said. "This might be a bad sign."

The staff laughed. The kind joke, intended to lessen my obvious embarrassment, had the opposite effect on me. Flustered, I pulled my arm out again and then jammed it down the sleeve, hoping for the best.

Out came my hand through the end of the sleeve. The staff cheered.

"Whew," I said. "This judging isn't easy," and there was general laughter.

I remember only a few details from those first cases. Horrified, I watched the judge step off the platform and walk to his robing room. He wasn't about to guide me through, he was just taking a break. I remember the court officer saying to me, "We'll do a couple of easy ones, Judge."

I did two domestic violence cases in which the accused decided to speak for themselves instead of being represented by lawyers (I intoned "respondent waives counsel" as though propounding a major new rule of law) and agreed to one-year protective orders against themselves. The orders prohibited acts against their wives that would represent the crimes of assault, menacing, reckless endangerment, harassment, or disorderly conduct. Violation could bring six months in jail.

The next respondent wanted a lawyer. I asked him questions to determine if he qualified for a court-appointed (taxpayer-paid) lawyer. No written criteria exist for qualification; this fellow took home $350 per week. I told him he would have to hire his own lawyer for the next court date.

"But, Judge, I can't afford a lawyer," he said to me.

"Well, you don't qualify for a free lawyer, sir."

"That's not fair."

The clerk leaned towards me. "Want me to get him out of here, Judge?"

I didn't want to appear to lose control. I whispered to the clerk, "I'll take care of it," and summoning a stern voice said, "Sir, you may step out now. Bring a lawyer if you want to be represented by counsel on the adjourned date. October fifth. Temporary order of protection is continued."

"Please step out," the court officer said to the two litigants. They turned and left. The clerk turned to me, "You're going to be fine, Judge. You've got the voice."

The other judge returned. I stood and took off his robe.

"So?" he asked.

"Piece of cake," I said. He laughed sardonically, the laugh of wisdom.

I breathed deeply, feeling as though I might faint. I had judged. Let the days begin.

A.M.

Tuesday morning. Exhausted after a bad night's sleep, I have a quick shower, make a stab at the day's clothes, and say a not-too-hopeful "right" to Laura's jocular "Be a good judge" on my way out the apartment door.

After two stops for take-out coffee and a *New York Times,* I march to my parking spot before an eight o'clock street-cleaning violation—a fifty-dollar ticket—finds its way to my car windshield. But not to complain. The Bronx Family Court and Bronx Criminal Court share a courthouse, which features a parking garage for judges and a few lucky support staff; thus I avoid stashing my beat-up subcompact in a $400 per month Manhattan garage.

The five-mile ride to the South Bronx takes just twenty minutes, another bonus of my assignment. I drive along the Grand Concourse and turn right on 163rd Street, then turn again behind the courthouse and drive down the ramp into the garage to my parking spot. In the garage I wait for an elevator to take me upstairs. The elevators are notorious for going up when signaling down and vice versa. This morning there's a different problem. The elevator arrives at the garage level, goes ding! as the up arrow lights above the door, then leaves without opening for me. I shift in place, reading a handwritten sign taped to the wall between the two sets of elevator doors. The sign says, WHAT? Roach/rodent extermination. WHEN? Today. WHAT TIME? 6 P.M.

Beneath the words "Roach/rodent" someone has added "to wit: judges, lawyers, caseworkers."

On its third try, the elevator decides to retrieve me and, finally, I make the ride to chambers. Feeling wasted, I start a pot of strong coffee. Last night was pure misery. Awaking all of a sudden just before two, I had begun a mental replay of one of yesterday afternoon's cases, an arraignment of a juvenile delinquency case.

The scene: At 5:30 I am presiding over the last of seven consecutive arraignments. Another dozen cases remain—emergency domestic violence cases—and the clerk of the part has obtained permission from court administration for thirty more minutes of overtime for the courtroom staff.

"Calling number 112 on the assignment calendar, Your Honor, in the matter of Holton," intones a uniformed court officer, who hands the case papers up to me at the bench. Then, sotto voce, he says, "The mother is the complaining witness on this one, Judge. You want to appoint a *guardian ad litem?*"

An unusual wrinkle, this. The accused juvenile's own mother as the crime victim. I glance at the case papers, which allege that the child assaulted Mom at home. The mother walks into the courtroom. She's tall and well-dressed, with a nasty shiner on her right eye. The man accompanying her turns out to be her husband, the accused's stepfather. Since the mother is the complainant, I need to appoint someone else as *guardian ad litem* for the child in court.

"I'll appoint 18-B," I tell the court officer, pointing to a lawyer sitting in the back of the courtroom awaiting appointment to cases. These appointments pay forty dollars per hour—"18-B" refers to the section of New York's County Law authorizing their assignment.

A New York City Legal Aid Society lawyer—defense counsel—steps up from the back of the courtroom as well. The full cast has assembled: the court stenographer and the liaison worker from the New York City probation department below me to my left at the side of the raised judge's bench; a city prosecutor, the mother, the stepfather, the 18-B lawyer as guardian, the juvenile defendant (called "respondent" in Family Court), and the Legal Aid defense lawyer standing from left to right at a table fifteen feet in front of me. A court officer stands directly behind the juvenile, another takes a position a bit farther back and to the respondent's left. While Legal Aid is entering a "denial" (Family Court jargon for a plea of not guilty) on behalf of his client, I stare at the respondent. She's fourteen, short, with a round face. She looks tense. In fact, she seems ready to blow.

"Your Honor," the prosecutor says, "I'm asking that you inquire of the mother regarding the status of the respondent pending trial. She has some information that I believe the Court would want to hear."

"I object, Your Honor," Legal Aid says immediately.

"Would counsel approach, please," I say to the two lawyers.

Off the record, at the bench, I ask, "What's going on?" and the prosecutor, looking grave, tells me that the mother wants to describe her daughter's recent suicidal, assaultive behavior at home, including an attempt last night to jump from their fifth-floor apartment window.

"I suggest a short E," the prosecutor adds, referring to a brief evaluation that the Family Court's mental health clinic would perform at my direction. Immediately following the evaluation, the clinic psychologist would provide a recommendation as to short-term care.

"You know better than that, it's after five o'clock," I tell the prosecutor. "The clinic's closed. If the mother's story sounds credible, I'm putting the kid in BCPC."

The reference is to Bronx Children's Psychiatric Center. I turn to the child's lawyer.

"Your client looks like she's going to explode."

The Legal Aid lawyer replies immediately. "Your Honor, there shouldn't be any psychiatric hospitalization at all. Look at my client's face. The mother assaulted her. I ask that you order pictures to be taken of my client to preserve the injuries for the record."

"I don't agree," I tell the lawyer. "Step back and we'll proceed. You can make whatever record you want."

When they are back at the table, I ask the mother, "What is it that you want to say, ma'am?" and she starts an awful tale of insanity at home.

"Your Honor, I object—" Legal Aid interrupts after five or six seconds.

"Counsel, please—"

"You're lying, you motherfucker!" the daughter yells.

Thinking about it in bed, I realize I should have had the third court officer escort the mother from the courtroom as soon as I finished the conference at the bench. I knew where the case was heading by then, and the 18-B guardian was in the courtroom for the child. The mother's presence wasn't required for any purpose. Yet, I hadn't thought to excuse her. It was an unusual arraignment, to be sure; next time I'd know better.

Now, in an attempt to end the daughter's outburst and gain control of the situation, I quickly say, "Based on the report of the respondent's mother, and on the respondent's outburst and my own observations of the respondent's appearance and demeanor in the courtroom, I find that the respondent is a danger to herself and others and requires psychiatric evaluation pending further proceedings. She is remanded for psychiatric evaluation and observation for a period of no more than fifteen days."

From behind the respondent, a court officer tries to take custody of the girl for the trip to the hospital. But the girl has already darted behind the 18-B lawyer and her stepfather. With her right fist she punches her mother on the left cheek.

The mother howls. Two other court officers join the fray and, restraining the girl, start moving her to a cell behind the courtroom. Chairs fall over at the counsel table. Mom shrieks. "I love you. I love you. My baby! Oh God!" Her husband puts his arms around her. The kid is shouting "You'll never take me! Fuck you!" as she is dragged out.

I watch, dumbfounded, a surge of adrenalin shooting through me. Then I turn to the court stenographer, who records my statement to her. "The record should reflect that the respondent has just assaulted her mother by punching her in the face." I put the statement on the record in the event the child's lawyer files a writ of habeas corpus to free the girl from the hospital.

For the judge deciding the writ, the clearer the picture of the courtroom scene the better.

I stand and walk off to my right, to my robing room, removing myself from the commotion. Closing the door, I sit at the robing room desk, listening to the shrieks and moans as the girl and her mother are moved out. In the detention cell, I will soon learn, the girl tries to strangle herself with the drawstrings of her sweatshirt hood.

After a few minutes, it's time to resume. I get back on the bench to process the domestic violence cases, including one in which one of my fellow citizens had put a gun to his pregnant girlfriend's head. By six o'clock I'm finished, in more ways than one.

In the middle of the night, I construct scenarios for similar cases in the future. Then, giving up on sleep, I put on a bathrobe and watch television for a few hours. I jot down several 800 numbers from the TV pitchmen: two sports magazine subscriptions are available, one with a complimentary Larry Bird highlights tape, the other with a tape of baseball's fifty greatest home runs. To pique my interest, they show the black-and-white film of Bobby Thompson's home run against the Brooklyn Dodgers in the 1951 playoff: "the shot heard 'round the world." I had listened to it as a child on radio as it happened that October afternoon, the Giants win the pennant, the Giants win the pennant, the Giants win the pennant. . . . And my friend Eddie the Dodger fan is sitting on the curb down the block, crying. . . .

I was a Yankee fan. I get back into bed and start to doze, thinking of simpler days.

Now, drinking coffee and scanning the *Times* a few hours later in chambers, I relish the privacy and quiet. After a while, I walk down the hall to check yesterday's mail. At the mailbox cubbyholes, I meet several Criminal Court judges whose names I still don't know. We exchange greetings, check the mail, and go our separate ways. In my mail is the daily *New York Law Journal*. I read the front-page headlines on the way back to chambers, then check the one-sentence summaries in the "Opinions of Note" box. I pour another cup of coffee and try to continue with the *Times*, but it's nine o'clock and I find myself thinking about the day ahead in Part 15. Ordinarily, court starts at 9:30, but today's calendar includes an adoption case. In Bronx Family Court, adoptions are completed before the day's main events.

I put on my suit jacket and head towards the elevator. Halfway down the hall, Judge Stallworth's door is open. I stick in my head to say good morning.

"Hey, Rose."

"Good morning, Rick. How's it going?"

"I don't know yet," I tell her, and she laughs.

"I had a weird one yesterday in intake," I tell her then and take her through yesterday's scene. I like getting feedback from Rose, who is in her seventeenth year on the bench. She has a solid legal grasp and good practical sense.

When I finish, she says, "Too bad it was so late, otherwise you could have sent the kid for the short E. Then you might have had an easier time with her after. That's always a tough situation. I wouldn't feel bad about it. The main thing is you did the right thing with her."

"How's your day look?" I ask her.

"I'm starting with sixty-two cases." She rolls her eyes. "I'm having a lot of trouble lately getting things started at 9:30. Yesterday I sat there until 10:15. I had a 9:30 call with Jackson [naming a lawyer] and she calls and says she's going to be late. Shows up at almost eleven."

"Did she say why?"

"I don't know. She was sick or something."

"Why don't you fine her?"

She looks at me. Suddenly I feel like a real rookie.

"You can't sanction everyone," she says. "She told me she was sick. I save fines for the really outrageous ones."

"I guess so," I tell her. "Well, I'd better get down to the part. I have an adoption."

I walk to the elevator and press the down button, then walk into a corridor nearby and press the button for the freight elevator, too. The regular elevator comes first and I ride to the seventh floor. Turning left, I walk along the corridor towards Part 15, feeling uneasy. After so much judging and thousands upon thousands of case appearances, the morning nerves are still there. It's worse this morning when I've hardly slept, despite the three cups of caffeine working on me.

At the end of the corridor I turn left and the robing room door to Part 18 is in front of me. The door is open. A Part 18 court officer is inside.

"Good morning, Judge," he says to me.

"Good morning," I say and decide to use the bathroom in the robing room there. The Part 15 robing room doesn't have a bathroom. When nature calls, the Part 15 judge leaves the courtroom, robed, and uses the bathroom in Part 18. Everyone knows why the judge is leaving, and on a major coffee day the urge might strike more than once or twice. I had expected the lack of privacy that comes with sitting in plain view on the bench all day, but not this hour-to-hour public knowledge of my private needs.

I walk through the corridor maze to my part. Early on, it had taken me weeks to learn to make the quick left-right-left turns between Part 15 and Part 18 automatically. On several occasions, turning incorrectly, I would have to double back in view of court officers near the prisoner detention cells between the courtrooms, feeling humiliated. Of course, the court officers probably hadn't given it two thoughts, having experienced over the years the adjustment pains of more new judges than they cared to recall.

Walking through the open side door to my part, the first person I see is my regular court officer, Bob, clipboard in hand, checking a case file on the table in front of the judge's bench. The files are arranged in rows according to case type and colored yellow, orange, or pink accordingly. With a glance at the table, one can tell with reasonable accuracy the demands of the day's calendar. In the upper left-hand corner of each file, Bob has penciled a number that corresponds to the case's number on the printed court calendar.

"Good morning, Judge," Bob says.

"Hi, Bob. Looks bad."

"You might be right. Let's hope for the best."

"Is Jane here yet? I've got that adoption."

Jane is the adoptions clerk. Bob says, "She's in the waiting room. The lawyer's here. You know, you've got a 9:30 call on a paternity case. Is that on for trial? I couldn't tell from the endorsement."

"No. Just for the lawyers. It's on for a motion. That's the one with the three brothers."

Bob laughs. "Oh, I remember that one. Two of the brothers are trying to get the third brother to take a blood test."

"Right. Are the lawyers here yet?"

"One of them. Perez."

"Well, let's see if we can do that one after the adoption."

"OK," Bob says, and heads back into the public waiting area.

I look around the courtroom. No portrait-walled, mahogany-paneled, hardwood-pewed chamber of justice, this Part 15. In fact, the space—only twenty-one by thirty-one feet—had been a records storage room. File cabinets still line a side wall towards the rear of the room. The off-white walls need painting. At the rear wall is a cramped area for lawyers awaiting the call of their cases. An array of chairs surrounds the government-issue table used by litigants and lawyers fifteen feet from the judge's bench. The furniture looks as though it had fallen from the back of a Goodwill truck at the end of a day's pickups, then scooped up for use in court. Walking over to the table, I grab two of the chairs and shake them. They would survive another day. New chairs were on order.

At the corner of the courtroom's business end is the robing room, a small cubicle, seven by nine feet, with a metal desk, four chairs, and a telephone. Tacked up on the rear wall is a cartoon in which a lawyer, looking up at a judge on the bench, calls the judge a "bald-headed, pea-brained coot." On another wall is a large calendar with black printing on a plain white background. Sheets of paper with telephone numbers of other courtrooms, agency offices, courthouse staff, and lawyers are stacked in a pile on the desk near the telephone on top of an ancient Bronx Yellow Pages. In addition to lacking a bathroom, the Part 15 robing room lacks a closet. I hang my suit jacket on a coat tree in the corner of the room and put on my robe. Along the bottom of the robe are blotches of dust from the robing room floor. As I spread the robe on the desk and rub at the dust, I decide I'll bring the robe to the dry cleaners on Sheridan Avenue at lunch hour. For a day or two I can use my dress robe, which, unfortunately, is made of much heavier material.

From inside the robing room, I can hear the human traffic in the waiting area. This particular quadrant of the waiting area serves four courtrooms. Mine is the noisiest. The entrance to Part 15 is at the end of a small hallway (called the "well") that connects the waiting area to the courtroom. In that hallway is the women's public bathroom. Worse, the busy room in which the public meets with court staff to have their cases typed for court processing (the "petition room") is located in this quadrant. The noisy, crowded waiting area jangles with the stuff of jammed-up lives. Coming to court is nobody's idea of a morning; outside my courtroom, the citizenry is cranky and burdened with special problems. Their little ones cling to them or play noisily about. More than a few who wait are confused at best and frightened at worst. Not infrequently, the waiting area erupts with emotional or physical surprise.

Back in the courtroom, three other staff have arrived. Near the bench, the court stenographer is setting up his stenotype machine. The crew of Family Court stenographers rotates daily through the parts, performing the tough job of keying every word of every case into their machines.

"Good morning, Dan," I say to him.

"How're you doing, Judge," he says, arranging his pads of transcription papers.

The clerk of the part, Ethel, has taken her position at a small desk to the right of the bench. At the end of each case appearance during the day, the clerk translates the judge's case notes (called "endorsements") into formal orders for the judge to review and sign. Some judges sign their orders in batches—a batch, say, before breaking for lunch and a batch at the end of the day. My style was to sign each order as the day progressed; I didn't like paper piling up for review. The clerk also annotates the case files and a copy of the part's printed court calendar to indicate the outcome of each case. These notes, which are based on a set of standard abbreviations for the variety of case outcomes, are entered the next day into the court's computerized case records. And vouchers for payment of the 18-B lawyers were filed following the completion of their cases; these awaited the part clerk's scan of the case file to verify the voucher entries. (I tried to sign the vouchers within a day or two after the lawyers submitted them.) And when the phone rang in the robing room—an event that required prompt response because it disrupted my concentration on the bench—the clerk (or a court officer) would go in to answer the call.

A former court officer who had passed the civil service examination for court clerk, Ethel was quick and energetic, moving the paperwork efficiently, helping with the phones, and keeping the day moving along in a variety of other subtle ways. Best of all, she could read my handwriting.

Angela, another uniformed court officer, had been working in the part for less than two weeks and I'd been pleased with her performance, though she wasn't as experienced as Bob. Bob was a gem, as effective and helpful as they get. His assignment to me was a piece of good fortune. Court officers determine the degree of a courthouse's efficiency and order; moreover, they can make or break a judge's day. All of the different types of court staff are important in their own ways, of course; a court stenographer, for example, might be called upon at any moment to read back testimony in court or might be ordered to produce a transcript of the hearing on short notice. But the court officer's influence is pervasive. The degree of security, order, and quiet in the courtroom; the quality of a judge's information about the availability of litigants and attorneys for cases; the flow of prisoners from detention cells and of interpreters and probation staff from their offices; the control of the courtroom door as attorneys check the readiness of their cases; the quality and speed of the metal detector weapons screening in the courthouse lobby; the nature of responses to disputes; fights and other kinds of disruption in waiting areas and the building lobby; the one-on-one protection of judges who have received threatening mail or phone calls; even the summoning of attorneys who may be tardy or otherwise derelict in answering the call of their cases—these are just a few of the tangible ways the court officers control the safety and efficiency of the day.

In Family Court relationships among the officers and judges were by and large cordial. The officers gave terrific service.

"What did you think of that scene in intake yesterday?" I ask Angela. She is standing at the end of the counsel table, making notations on her calendar to share with Bob about lawyers and litigants in the waiting area.

Angela shakes her head. "That was really sad, Judge. You know she tried to strangle herself in detention."

"I know. Really awful. You could tell right away she was very tense."

"I didn't see her when she was brought in. I couldn't understand that lawyer. I mean, saying the kid should go home—"

"Well, he had a client to represent," I reply, keeping my response ambiguous, and fall silent, trying to observe the bounds of proper judicial comment.

Angela says, "Jane's ready with the adoption, Judge."

"OK, bring it in."

Here is a start to a morning any judge enjoys: Into the courtroom on adoption mornings comes Auntie, or Grandma, or a nonrelative who over years of foster parenting has become the child's real parent. In hand is an adorable toddler, or just-school-age boy or girl dolled up in Sunday best and looking cherubic.

The adoptive parent is nervous, but these are not the nerves of the more typical Family Court litigant involved in child custody, domestic violence, child neglect, or juvenile delinquency proceedings. This occasion is a happy one; after the two-minute courtroom script is played out, the judge approves the adoption, there are smiles and tears and, not infrequently, picture-taking with the new parent and child and the judge in robes. Then the courtroom empties and the judge and staff prepare for the day's meaner stuff.

Sometimes, though, adoptions had strange outcomes. Consider the Case of the Two Mothers. Tossed before me one busy afternoon, the case papers indicated a request for custody of a fifteen-year-old boy by a woman described in the petition as an "unrelated caretaker." The respondent, or current legal custodian of the child, was described on the papers as "the mother."

"Your name and relationship to the child?" the court officer asked the petitioner in the courtroom.

The petitioner gave her name and said, "I'm his mother."

I took another glance at the papers. Meanwhile, the respondent gave her name and said, "I'm his mother."

The court officer looked at me and shrugged. My court clerk muttered, "Good luck, Judge."

Was this the Family Court's version of *To Tell the Truth*? Did *60 Minutes* have a hidden camera on one woman's lapel? Had the clerk typing the case papers made a mistake? Suddenly, I had an attentive audience of a dozen or so court officers, clerks, and lawyers in the courtroom: an irresistible opportunity for a judicial one-liner.

"Well," I said to the two of them, looking across the courtroom at one, then the other, "will the real mother please stand up?"

This got a chuckle from the onlookers but no response from the litigants.

"Ma'am, this petition that you filed says you are unrelated to the child, yet you just said you are the mother. What's going on?"

"I'm his natural mother. That's my sister." Mom #1 pointed at the respondent.

"You're the child's aunt, Ma'am?" I asked the respondent.

"Well, yes, Your Honor," Mom #2 said.

"Let me guess," I said to the aunt. "You adopted your sister's child."

"That's right, Your Honor."

"So you are in fact the child's mother, right?"

"I'm really his aunt," Mom #2 said.

"How long ago did you adopt him?"

"Four years ago."

"Where did the adoption take place?"

"In Brooklyn. I was living there then."

"Was there a case in Brooklyn Family Court involving this child prior to the adoption?"

Mom #1 spoke up, "No, Judge. I surrendered the child out of court. The agency said I should give him up because I was having problems at the time."

"What agency?"

She named a foster care agency.

"How did you get involved with the agency?"

"I was involved with drugs. I placed my son in foster care voluntarily so I wouldn't have to come to court. Then the agency said I should surrender him so my sister could adopt him. It seemed like a good idea at the time."

Was her last line a joke? I looked at her again.

"Well, did you know what you were doing when you surrendered the child? Did anyone force you, or mislead you in any way?"

"No."

"Did they tell you when you surrendered the child out of court that after a certain period of time you couldn't sue for custody ever again?"

"I don't remember."

"Where is the child living now?"

"My son has been back with me for the last four months," Mom #1 said.

I was taking too long with this, considering the day's heavy calendar. Yet I needed to pursue more facts.

Over time, I had learned to tread carefully around the parental surrender as a device for terminating irrevocably a parent's rights regarding a child. Once the parent signs a "surrender instrument," as Mom #1 had in this case, the child is "freed for adoption," as the expression goes. That is, the parent's consent to the child's adoption is no longer required. The child's mother is no longer the legal mother, the child's father is no longer the legal father, and the parents can never regain the right to have legal custody of the child.

In New York, a parent can surrender a child out of court before witnesses or in court before a Family Court judge. While an out-of-court surrender provides a short grace period (forty-five days) within which the parent can revoke the surrender, a surrender before a judge is irrevocable upon the signing of the surrender instrument. The parent signs four copies at the courtroom table or in the robing room in the presence of the judge, surrounded, in the ordinary case, by a foster care agency caseworker, a lawyer assigned to the parent, a court clerk, and a notary public. Then the judge signs and the parent is no longer Mom or Dad.

What was the appropriate judicial comment at that point? "Congratulations"? "Thank you"? "Next case"? I've never figured it out.

From the practical standpoint of calendar management, surrenders can be troublesome. Clerks and court officers usually wince when they tell a judge "We've got a surrender coming in." In the first place, there is all that paperwork. Secondly, the proceedings commonly take at least twenty minutes to complete—if all goes smoothly. Sometimes, a parent breaks down or experiences a change of heart during the series of questions a judge must ask prior to deciding whether to approve the surrender. I ask sixteen standard questions, among them: Do you realize you are entitled to financial aid or services such as counseling that might help you to avoid the need for this surrender? Has anyone made a threat of any kind to force you to surrender your child? Has anyone promised you anything in exchange for this surrender? Has anyone given you money or any other thing of value, or promised to give you money or any other thing of value, in exchange for this surrender? Are you surrendering this child of your own free will and only because you want to and for no other reason? Do you realize that once I approve this surrender you will no longer be the mother (father) of this child for any purpose? Do you understand that your surrender will be effective immediately and you cannot change your mind thereafter? Do you want to surrender your child?

In receiving the parent's answers to these and other questions, a judge is looking for signs of hesitation, lack of understanding of the process or the consequences, or other indication that the parent does not truly want to, or ought not, surrender the child—at least at that day's hearing. A common practice is to adjourn the case for several weeks so that the parent can think it over. Some judges adjourn all surrenders at least once for that purpose. Occasionally, parents ready to surrender today disappear tomorrow or simply get cold feet about giving up their rights.

And then there is the so-called conditional surrender. New York law permits the surrendering parent to name the person who will adopt the child. If that person doesn't adopt, the parent's rights are fully restored as though never given up at all. In the Case of the Two Mothers, for example, Mom #1, the natural mother, had designated her sister, Mom #2, who in fact subsequently adopted the child. Consider, then, the ordinary underlying situation of a conditional surrender: the natural parent relinquishes, in theory, his or her rights to the child but retains, as a matter of law, the right to choose the child's next parent.

Back to the Case of the Two Mothers. My inquiry revealed that the fifteen-year-old had never settled in at the aunt's house, spending large chunks of time at his natural mother's house, despite her surrender, during his four years as his aunt's adopted child. Five months prior to the filing of Mom #1's custody case, he had moved out of his aunt's house for good.

"Why did he leave?" I asked Mom #2.

The aunt shrugged. "He didn't like it with me."

"Why not?" I tried again.

"He was always hard to control."

Not much of a response to the question. While the aunt seemed evasive, the line of inquiry was pointless. By this stage, I probably wasn't going to order state child protective action based on the aunt's conduct; this was a teenager who had no intention of living with her. I looked at Mom #1.

"Why did you wait five months before coming to court for custody once the child returned to you for good?" I asked her.

"My unemployment ran out a few weeks ago."

"Aha!" I said, trying to form an appropriately withering facial expression, then realized I was moving out of line. Mom #1 stared at me, entirely unaware of any wrongdoing.

And, in fact, she was guilty of none. Her voluntary placement of the child into foster care with her sister, her parental
surrender, and her sister's state-subsidized adoption represented behavior and status changes that were perfectly legal.
Now, unemployment benefits exhausted, Mom #1 needed a
court custody order to obtain welfare benefits under Aid for
Dependent Children. The order was necessary because she was
no longer the legal parent; the aunt was.

"I'm curious about something," I said to Mom #1 now. "Did
you register the child in school this fall? Or did your sister?"

"I did."

"How did you manage that without custody papers?"

"I showed them his old birth certificate. I'm still his mother
on that."

"Well, ma'am, I can't grant you custody. You gave up the
legal right to custody when you surrendered the child."

"So what do you suggest I do?"

"I suggest you consult with the child's parent." I looked
over at the aunt, "You did adopt him, did you not, ma'am?"

"Well—"

"This case is dismissed. You still have a drug problem?" I
said to Mom #1.

"No."

"Do you intend to provide care for this child?" I asked the
aunt.

"Not really."

"Child Welfare Agency investigation is ordered. CWA is to
take appropriate action as may be indicated to protect the
child's well-being."

I wrote "Dismissed, oral decision on record" on the case endorsement sheet and handed the papers to the clerk. The two Moms didn't move. The court officer said, "Step out, please." Obviously, they were having difficulty getting the point.

However intriguing this case was from a factual standpoint, my view of it from the bench was straightforward: Mom #1 gave up her right to sue for custody when she signed the surrender instrument; therefore, I could not consider the substantive issue of what was in the best interests of the child. Frustrating, since the child seemed to have a relationship with his natural mother and not his aunt, but my hands were tied because of the surrender.

The phrase "best interests of the child" appears several dozen times in New York State laws governing support, custody, visitation, adoption, and protection of children. The meaning of these phrases, and the criteria judges are supposed to use in determining case outcomes under this standard, are set forth in thousands of appellate court and trial court decisions. No legal principle, and certainly no amount of written words, however, provide better guidance as to a child's best interests than good common sense. Family Court judges ultimately try to stick to what seems practical and sensible.

And so with this morning's first case. From the case papers, I felt that the proposed adoption was not in the child's best interests. I step up on the platform of the raised bench and sit down in my orange soft-cushioned swivel chair. I had moved the chair from chambers to replace the narrower, stiffer model I found when I arrived. The orange color is hideous but the chair is comfortable, the only thing that matters now that I am glued to it all week. Seated at the bench, I look out at the lawyer for the proposed adoptive parent, who is the six-year-old girl's grandmother. The grandmother isn't in the courtroom.

"Mr. Kleinfeld, I notice your client isn't here this morning," I say to him.

"Well, Your Honor, I didn't think she was needed. I understood from your law clerk that you wanted to discuss with me problems you have with the adoption."

"Well, Mr. Kleinfeld, I've done a thorough review of the documents submitted in support of the adoption, and I would deny the petition based on those. Before I rule, though, Mr. Kleinfeld, I wanted to ask you if there is anything else you intend to add to the record. If so, you can do that today or if you want an adjournment for that purpose, I will grant it. For example, if you want your client to present testimony or other evidence. Then I would consider the entire record."

"No, there's nothing, Judge."

"Then I'll rule at this time. As you know, Mr. Kleinfeld, the mother of this child is serving a prison sentence for beating to death the child's sister. Your client is the maternal grandmother. The child has frequent contact with her mother when your client takes her to the prison where her mother is incarcerated. The grandmother stated quite candidly in her affidavit that she intends to continue these visits and to encourage a continuing relationship between the child and her mother. Your client also intends to have the child keep her mother's surname, which is different from your client's, after the adoption. Finally, the natural mother will be eligible for parole while the child is still relatively young; she continues to deny responsibility for the death of her other daughter, blaming it on her former boyfriend.

In these circumstances, I do not believe that the intent of the Domestic Relations Law, which in essence defines an adoption as the permanent substitution of one parent for another, would be fulfilled by granting this adoption. In reality, I view your client's caretaking plan and her solution to the family situation as a temporary custody arrangement under which the credible evidence shows she will care for the child until the mother is out of prison. Moreover, given the mother's denial of guilt for the murder of her daughter, I do not believe that ending foster care supervision of this family is wise at this time. Careful monitoring of the mother's emotional and psychological condition will be necessary if and when she is out on parole and resumes un-supervised contact with this child. For these reasons, the grandmother's petition to adopt is denied."

The lawyer says, "Please note my exception, Your Honor. Have a good day." He puts a manila file into his attache case and heads for the courtroom door. The next week he will appeal my ruling.

I hand the case papers to the adoptions clerk. Then I say, "Thanks, Jane. Can you do me a favor? Ask Bob or Angela to come in."

"Sure, Judge, and have a good day," Jane says, and goes out into the waiting area.

Soon Angela returns. "Can you check on number 6?" I ask her. "The two lawyers on the paternity."

"Only Perez is here," Angela says. "But we've got a two-sider O we can do. Number 34."

"O" is the court records system's letter-prefix for domestic violence cases, which are known in New York law as "family offense" matters.

"Well, might as well get started. Go ahead and bring it in," I say to Angela.

"OK, Judge."

In a few moments a couple comes through the door, the woman first, followed by a stocky man in green slacks and a white T-shirt. Angela directs the petitioner (the woman who filed the case) to stand facing me to my left at the counsel table. The man, as the respondent, stands at the other end of the table. These are standard places for petitioners and respondents, making it easy to know who's who.

"Your Honor, number 34 on the Part 15 calendar, in the matter of Soto," Angela says and hands the case papers up to me.

"Raise your right hand," she says to them. "Do you swear to tell the truth—" She stops. "Your right hand, sir," she says to the man, who has raised his left (this happens at least five times a day), then, "Do you need an interpreter, sir?"

The man puts down his left hand and sticks up his right. We might have to stop to summon an interpreter from an office in the hallway behind the part. Since Angela can't leave me without security in the courtroom, I'm going to have to send Ethel to find Bob in the waiting area.

But the man says no, and Angela continues, "Do you swear to tell the truth so help you God?" They say yes and Angela says, "You may be seated."

I make a quick study of the key elements in the case papers: unmarried couple with a three-year-old daughter in common, they have different addresses. I had issued a temporary order of protection to the woman eight weeks ago. He had made a visit to her apartment and, she said, slapped her around.

This review takes five seconds.

Glancing at their names on the petition (having forgotten the name Angela used when she called the case), I say, "Ms. Rinton, Mr. Soto, you have the right to have lawyers to help you with this case. You can hire your own lawyer or, if you qualify, lawyers can be appointed for you free of charge. Or you can choose to speak for yourself this morning. Mr. Soto, which would you like to do?"

"Do I need a lawyer?"

"It's completely up to you, sir. I'm just letting you know what your rights are."

He hesitates, then, "I'll speak for myself."

"Ma'am?"

"Me too."

"Petitioner and respondent waive counsel," I say for the record, then continue, "Mr. Soto, you also have the right to have a hearing in this case and at that hearing these things you're said to have done would have to be proved to the court. And you would have the chance to tell your side of the story at that hearing and bring witnesses or other evidence to court. Or, if you wish, instead of having that hearing and without admitting that you did anything, you can agree to have a final order of protection issued against you. Do you know what an order of protection is?"

"No."

"It would provide that for a period of one year you would not assault this woman, harass, menace, or recklessly endanger her, or commit acts of disorderly conduct with respect to her, and that you would stay away from her home and the minor child except for any court-ordered visitation you may have. And if you violate that order and it is proved to the court that you did so, you could be jailed for up to six months. Now, do you understand what an order of protection is?"

"Yes."

"Do you want to have a full hearing or do you want to agree to a final order of protection?"

"Judge—" the woman starts to say.

I hold up my right hand. "One moment, please, ma'am."

"He wants to visit with our daughter."

"Please, ma'am. Visitation is a separate issue. Now, sir, how would you like to proceed?"

"Would the hearing happen right now?" the man asks.

"No, sir. The court's too busy today. The case would be put off to another date approximately eight weeks from today and the temporary order of protection would continue in effect until then."

"Well, I can't take another day to come here. I'll go along with the order of protection."

Immediately, for the record, I say, "On consent and without admission, a final order of protection is issued on the usual terms, and respondent is to stay away from petitioner's home and the minor child except for court-ordered visitation, if any," writing on my endorsement sheet "FOP UT+S/A exc. c/o vst."

Now the woman says, "About the visitation, Judge."

"Excuse me, ma'am." I turn to the man, "Were you two married, sir, or have you ever been declared the legal father of this child in court?"

"No."

"Did you sign any papers at the hospital when the child was born?"

"I wasn't at the hospital."

"Ma'am, is his name on the child's birth certificate?"

"No."

"Ma'am, right now this man has no legal right to visit the child. Wait outside the courtroom for your order of protection, please. And sir, if you want to file a case to be named the legal father of the child and seek a visitation order, the court staff will tell you how to do this. It's even possible I could consider those cases later today."

"Judge," the woman says now, "if you don't give him visitation he's not going to pay attention to the order of protection. I'd rather that he have the visitation."

"Ma'am, if he doesn't obey the order of protection, just call the police."

"By the time they get there it'll be too late, Judge," the woman says, sounding more resigned than frightened.

I turn to the man. "Sir, are you willing to file a case to have yourself named as the legal father of this child?"

"I'm not working now so I couldn't pay child support," he says. "I'm not letting myself in for that."

"Ma'am, this man has no visitation rights and I am not making any such orders unless and until he decides to accept his responsibilities and I am convinced it is safe for him to be around the child. These papers you filed say that he beat you up while your daughter was in the house, right?"

"He only slapped me a few times. I'd just as soon drop the order of protection than leave it like this."

"Well, I won't permit you to do that. I'm referring you to the Victim Services Agency. They'll counsel you on how to handle this situation and on how to use the order of protection."

To the man I say, "Sir, remember that I told you that a violation of the order of protection can land you in jail for up to six months. Please keep that in mind during the next year."

He says nothing, glaring at me.

"And as for child visitation, sir," I continue, "New York law considers acts of domestic violence to be important evidence indicating that visits with the violent parent may not be in the best interests of the child. If you file a case for visitation you should understand that this issue will be fully explored."

"I would never hurt my kid," the man replies.

"Violence towards the child's mother hurts the child badly, sir. And it is a sign to me of a serious problem with a parent's ability to control his or her behavior." Now I look over at Angela and nod my head.

"Step out, please," Angela tells the two litigants. They head for the door.

One down, a whole lot to go.

Bob returns. "The two lawyers are here on the 9:30 call. They're talking."

"They're talking" is code for lawyers trying to work out a settlement.

"I've got a no-service case, if you want to do it in the meantime."

"OK. Which number?"

"26."

I look at the calendar. The case is another domestic violence matter, in which the woman has failed to have the summons and temporary order of protection served on the respondent since the day she was first in court.

A young, short woman enters the courtroom, looking harried and with a toddler in her arms. Bob calls the case and administers the oath.

"You may be seated, ma'am," I tell her, and before she can sit I say to her (although I already know the answer), "Were you able to get these papers served on Mr. Washington?"

"No."

"Well, you're going to have to do that before I can consider giving you a final order of protection. Are you still seeking to go ahead with this case?"

"Yes."

"Judge, I didn't get what you said," the court stenographer says all of a sudden, his tone indicating irritation. "She was moving her chair."

I repeat myself for him; he keys it into his machine.

"Now, ma'am, do you know where this man is living? Is the address you gave for him on the court papers any good?"

"He hasn't lived there for a while."

"Well, ma'am, I'm going to keep the temporary order of protection going for two more weeks to give you a chance to get the papers served on him. If he comes around your building or if you see him on the street call the police and have them serve the papers. Don't do anything yourself. Does he have any relatives where he might hang out?"

"None that I know of."

I set an adjourned date two weeks out, looking at the size of my calendar for that day as shown on the scheduling device called the "control sheet." The control sheet, updated every day in the back office from entries made by the part clerk during the previous day, shows each judge's daily calendar size for the next three months.

"Please step out," Bob tells the woman. She retrieves her child from under the table where he's been exploring and leaves. As she goes, Bob hands her a slip of paper with the adjourned date on it. He'd inserted the date on the printed form as I was saying it, another court officer task.

Angela returns. She and Bob consult for a moment, making notes on their calendars.

"Let's see if the lawyers are ready on the paternity," I say to them. Bob goes out to the waiting area. The clerk hands me the final order of protection to sign from the first case. The order is a printed form with various options for the case dispositions permitted by the statute. I sign the order after the most cursory of glances, then force my mind to focus on the next case, which is going to require bringing to bear both law and tactics. Should I conference the case off the record in the robing room first? Bob has returned with the lawyers. I decide against the conference and go right on the record.

"Your Honor, number 6 on the Part 15 calendar, in the matter of Williams. Counsel, please note your appearances."

Bob hands me the endorsement sheet and the two privately hired lawyers identify themselves for the record.

In this paternity case, a woman (the petitioner) seeking financial support for a child from a recently ended five-year relationship has sued her ex-boyfriend to have him declared the father of a three-year-old girl. Previously I have ordered, at the parties' expense and with their consent, human leukocyte antigen (HLA) blood test analysis and DNA analysis. A lab takes blood samples from the petitioner, the respondent, and the child and reports the results: in this case, the report is that ex-boyfriend is 99.1 percent or 99.4 percent probably the father, depending on whether one is reading the HLA or the DNA analysis. (I am simplifying outrageously here.) Moreover, the woman has testified that she had sex with the boyfriend in the "early part" of June 1987; the child was born March 16, 1988. The birth certificate doesn't name a father.

On cross-examination, the woman has already testified to having had sex with her boyfriend's brother (Brother #2 for our purposes) on more than a few occasions during her relationship with Brother #1 and that the last time she had sex with Brother #2 was the first or second week of June 1987. The respondent (Brother #1, remember) now wants to introduce additional evidence and makes this "offer of proof": Brother #3, who owns a coffee shop in the Bronx and for whom the woman once worked as a waitress, will testify that the woman told him at the coffee shop on the morning of June 19, 1987 that she had been "out with" Brother #2 the night before, which explained why she was late for work that morning. Brother #1 will testify that the woman, in fact, did not come home until 5 A.M. on the morning of June 19, 1987.

In addition, Brother #1's lawyer wants me to order blood tests on the mother, the child, and Brother #2, which he argues will show that the probability of Brother #2's paternity is equal to or greater than that of his client's.

"This matter was put over to today," I start talking for the record, "for decision on respondent's motion to have the court order blood tests on respondent's brother and also for scheduling of the completion of the trial, which has reached the point where respondent's case would go forward. Does that reflect your understanding as well, Counsel?"

They both agree.

"As for the motion," I continue, looking at petitioner's lawyer, "I have not received answering papers from petitioner's counsel as of today. Have you filed them?"

"Not yet, Your Honor. I apologize for being a bit late with them. I was planning to have them filed by the end of today."

"Well, then, I am going to wait to decide the motion until I review those. In addition, I am going to give respondent's counsel a small amount of additional time to bring forth legal authority in support of his motion. That was lacking in your submission, Counselor," I say to him, a smidgen of rebuke in my voice, "which mainly made a factual and practical argument as opposed to a legal one. Moreover, I would like respondent to put on his case before I decide the motion."

There is little if anything that they can say to this. I continue, "Now as to the offer of proof regarding what petitioner may have said to respondent's brother about sexual relations with the other brother, this would be admissible as an admission of a party-opponent. However, I am asking you, Mr. Silver, with respect to other evidence that you may be seeking to introduce, to review Section 531 of the Family Court Act and the related caselaw on the admissibility, in the absence of corroborating evidence, of testimony regarding the petitioner's access to other alleged sexual partners. And that's all I want to say about that."

"I understand, Your Honor," the respondent's lawyer says.

"Now was there anything else either of you wanted to raise before we pick a date for completion of the trial?"

There wasn't. Looking at them, I have a sense they are surprised by how directive I have been. Am I coming on too hard? I wonder. I haven't had enough sleep, after all, I've got dozens more cases to do, and this case has me somewhat uptight. Am I going to name the wrong father? Or cheat this kid out of a father that is really hers? How on earth am I going to decide this crazy case? And where's my shared half a law clerk this morning, anyway?

We pick a date ten weeks hence for the rest of the trial. The lawyers leave, grateful to have finished with the case early in the day and without a long delay in the waiting area before the case was called.

Bob comes over.

"That was quick," he says. "I talked to Johnson. He's ready on the Mapp, but he's not going to have his witness on the other D. I told him to wait around while we got Mr. Gold. He told me he's in Part 3. The kid's here with his mother."

A "Mapp" is a hearing, named after the United States Supreme Court case of *Mapp v. Ohio,* to determine if a police seizure of evidence was legal. Johnson was the New York City assistant corporation counsel—the Family Court equivalent of an assistant district attorney—prosecuting the crack possession case. Gold was an 18-B lawyer. His client was in the waiting area with Mom. The other delinquency case (the "D," as Bob had called it), the one not ready for trial, involved an alleged assault that was supposed to have taken place on a bus.

"As long as we have Johnson, let's see if we can get Ms. Stoddard over here, too. We can do both cases."

"OK, Judge," Bob says, and then Angela says something to him that I can't hear. Bob turns to me and says, "There's a one-sider O with service we can do."

"Is the line finished?" I ask him.

"I think so. Angela will call."

Angela goes into the robing room to call the officers downstairs in the courthouse lobby. If the line going through the metal detectors still has people on it, I'd be better off not doing the one-sider yet. The other party to the case might appear in the waiting room soon after, raising the issue of whether I should reopen the case. The petitioner would have to be notified to come back to court. Yet, court summonses are for 9:30 A.M. unless otherwise noted; one of the strengths of Bronx Family Court was that all of the judges, without exception, were diligent about taking the bench at 9:30. How much tardiness should judges excuse in litigants?

But Angela reports the line has finished. I ask her to bring the petitioner into the courtroom. Within a minute I am pronouncing, "The affidavit of service is made part of the record for the purpose of disposition. Based on the petitioner's testimony and the respondent having defaulted, a final order of protection is issued on standard terms."

Bob is conferring with Angela. I ask them what's going on.

"I called Legal Aid," Angela says. "Stoddard is on her way over. Gold, too. We can do the Mapp and the other one."

"Good work. How'd you manage that?"

Angela laughs. "Also, there are three two-sider V's out there. You want Elaine to conference them?" she asks, naming my law clerk.

"V" is the Family Court's letter-prefix for child custody and visitation cases. A "two-sider" means that both the petitioner and the respondent (Mom and Dad) have shown up for the case.

"Have you seen Elaine?"

"No."

"Well, she should definitely start conferencing them, if you see her."

The courtroom door opens and in come Johnson, Gold, and Stoddard. We're ready to roll.

"Your Honor, calling number 9 on the Part 15 calendar, in the matter of Coleman," Angela says. A stocky fourteen-year-old kid and his mother join Johnson and Stoddard at the table. Gold sits in the back of the courtroom, awaiting his turn.

This is it, the last day of statutory speedy trial time. Either Johnson is ready to prove the case or the law requires that I dismiss it. Attached to the petition are the sworn depositions of the two complaining witnesses. They tell of a vicious, unprovoked physical assault on two fourteen-year-old girls on a city bus one afternoon. One girl had intervened after the respondent grabbed the other girl's breast.

The lawyers note their appearance. The respondent and his mother identify themselves and swear to tell the truth. Then I say, "Mr. Johnson, are you ready to proceed today?"

"No, Your Honor. The complaining witnesses have not appeared at this point."

"Do you expect them to appear today?"

"Well, I haven't been able to reach them. They don't have telephones and they haven't responded to a Mailgram that I sent."

"This is essentially the same situation that you presented to the court when the matter was last adjourned, isn't that right?"

"Yes, Your Honor. I would ask that the matter be recalled later today so that I can again try to contact my witnesses."

"Ms. Stoddard?"

"Your Honor, I ask that the matter be dismissed. These witnesses obviously aren't going to follow through with their complaint and I note this is the last day of speedy trial time. There is no good cause, as required by the Family Court Act, that would justify an adjournment."

Recalling the case after lunch was a stab in the dark, but still, if just one of the witnesses showed up, I could at least start the trial. This was a nasty (alleged) assault case, not one to be dismissed casually. Even at the end of the day, I could have a witness sworn; the prosecutor could begin questioning. That would satisfy the speedy trial requirement. I could finish the trial tomorrow.

Nah, I tell myself. The witnesses aren't coming, face it.

"The motion to dismiss is granted."

"Thank you, Your Honor," Stoddard says.

"Is that it, Judge?" Angela asks me. I nod.

"Parties, step out, please," Angela says. Stoddard whispers something to the kid and he nods. He and his mother leave. I stare at him as he goes, then make myself forget about it.

On to the Mapp hearing, which will require me to concentrate on the testimony, take good notes, make rulings on evidentiary objections, and deliver findings of fact, conclusions of law, and a decision immediately at the end of the hearing. I give Bob three dollars and ask him to call for coffee for me and the crew. The bodegas deliver; the coffee will arrive within fifteen minutes.

From a loose-leaf notebook among my law books on the bench, I find the decision outline I have prepared for Mapp hearings. The outline contains the basic structure and standard language of a Mapp decision. All that is missing is the hard part, the decision itself.

"Your Honor, calling number 18 on the Part 15 calendar, in the matter of Wilson," Angela says. "Mr. Gold, step up, please."

In a few moments a tall, rangy police officer, perhaps thirty years old and with a thick blonde moustache, is on the witness stand and the prosecutor is standing across from the witness. The prosecutor takes the cop through the details of a drug bust involving the fourteen-year-old respondent. Early in the testimony, defense counsel makes several incorrect objections to the prosecutor's questions. I overrule all of them and the objections stop. Using a separate line for every answer the cop gives, I scribble notes on a yellow pad as the cop testifies. I've been working on my handwriting; my clerk says it's the worst in the courthouse.

I get into a good concentration groove. Suddenly, the cop gives two consecutive responses that clearly represent inadmissible evidence and should be stricken from the hearing record. The cop testifies as to his impression of what the accused saw at the crime scene, instead of describing what he, the cop, observed. But the defense doesn't object. After the second answer, I stare at the young lawyer, as though inviting an objection. He stares back, saying nothing. I look away.

My coffee arrives, Ethel hands it to me. I pour the coffee into a blue ceramic cup, respecting my wife's observation that drinking from a take-out cup looks too informal on the bench. Between sips, I keep the cup out of sight behind a row of law books.

Soon the case's fact pattern is clear. The seizure of the fourteen vials of crack from the respondent, as well as the search of the respondent that yielded $117 from his pants pocket,

appear legal—if I take the cop at his word and if his testimony
stands up under cross-examination. But the cop's story is awfully pat, perhaps tailored to prove the legality of the search.

According to the cop's testimony, he is in the passenger
seat of a police car with his partner driving on routine patrol at
1:30 P.M. one Saturday. They approach a Bronx intersection that
is known to the police as a drug-dealing location. As they
approach, six to eight youths begin to disperse, some walking,
a few running. The police car pulls over, passenger side to the
curb. Out jumps the cop, moving quickly to the respondent,
who is one of the group who has started to walk rapidly away.
As the fourteen-year-old walks, he drops a handful of crack vials
to the ground, then puts his right hand to his mouth. The cop
moves close to the respondent and tells him to empty his mouth.
Out come crack vials. The cop places him under arrest, retrieves
the vials, and searches the respondent's pants, finding the cash.
The kid is charged with criminal possession of a dangerous drug
and criminal possession with intent to sell.

Cross-examination begins. The defense lawyer has no strat-
egy for attacking the direct testimony, merely leading the officer
through a rehash of his story. This takes time; I get impatient.
Worse, there are long pauses between questions. Finally, after
a particularly long pause, I say, as gently and blandly as I can
manage, "Mr. Gold, do you have any more questions?"

"Yes, Your Honor."

"Would you please ask one?" I reply, trying (hard) not to
sound impatient or sarcastic.

Mr. Gold hesitates, then says, "Your Honor, I'm reviewing
my notes. If I seem a little confused this morning, it's because
I have a terrible headache."

Good Lord.

I look over at Bob and Angela, who give resigned shrugs. The cop is less charitable. He snorts.

"Mr. Gold, are you certain you can provide adequate representation for your client this morning?" I ask now. "If you are too ill, I would grant your request for a continuance so that you may conduct your defense with your full capabilities."

"No, Your Honor. I just need a minute."

I assure him, "You may take whatever time you need. Are you sure you don't need a continuance?"

"I'm sure."

There are a few seconds of silence, followed by several more questions, then more silence.

"Mr. Gold?"

"One moment, Your Honor." More silence, and then, "That's all I have, Your Honor."

I excuse the officer, who leaves. Mr. Gold puts the kid on the witness stand. His mother had given him $120 that morning to buy clothes, he testifies. He was on his way to a store, stopped to have a few slices of pizza and hang out for a short time when the police drove up and arrested him for standing on the street. It was the other guys, whom he had never seen before, that had dropped the crack. The cop had lied about his putting the crack vials in his mouth; it had never happened. The kid handles the prosecutor's cross-examination pretty well, sticking with the crucial details of his story.

What is the truth? I wonder. The cop was an awfully smooth witness, too smooth, perhaps. Yet, the kid's story seems a total fabrication except maybe for the pizza purchase. Almost certainly the respondent was out there dealing, but the legality of the seizure of the cash depended on the legality of the seizure of the crack vials. Did the kid really drop them, or did someone else? Was the crack-vials-in-the-mouth story true?

Don't worry it to death, I tell myself. Going with my gut, I find the cop's testimony credible and deny the defense motion to suppress the drugs and cash as evidence at trial.

It is time to twist arms. "Counsel, may I see you in the robing room, please?" I say to them after reading my Mapp decision into the record.

In the robing room—off the record—I look at the defense lawyer. "Well?"

"Well, what, Your Honor?"

"Would you be prepared to accept an offer? Mr. Johnson, is there an offer?" I ask the prosecutor.

"We'd take a plea to just the possession, Judge."

"Mr. Gold? You're not going to take me through a trial on this same evidence, are you?"

"I need to talk to my client and his mother."

"Go right ahead."

Five minutes later, the case is over for today, the juvenile having made an admission (guilty plea) to the drug possession charge, a probation report having been ordered for the dispositional hearing (sentencing) six weeks from now, and the kid having been paroled to Mom in the meantime. When he allocutes (makes the admission), he admits to having had the crack on him. He's about to admit to selling the stuff, too, when his lawyer grabs his arm and tells him that he has said all he needs to. As he speaks, it's obvious he's telling the truth, this time around. I'd figured it right.

I drink the remaining third of my coffee, which is cold, then start for the Part 18 bathroom, when the court stenographer asks to take a break.

It's early for a break. "I'm just hitting the bathroom, Dan. I'll be back in a minute. Why don't you take a quick walk or something? But just for a couple of minutes."

When I get to the robing room in Part 18, there are six, count 'em, six lawyers in there. The three seats are taken and the other three lawyers are standing. No judge, though, he's in the courtroom. One of the lawyers sitting down is a corporation counsel for juvenile delinquency cases and two others are New York City Human Resource Administration Office of Legal Affairs (OLA) lawyers for child protective cases. An 18-B lawyer and two Legal Aid lawyers complete the picture. The 18-B lawyer is sitting on the judge's desk. His feet dangle above the floor. His casual behavior and demeanor irritate me.

I realize that I am looking at two combinations of lawyers for different cases, one set for a delinquency case, the other for a child neglect case, who are awaiting either a robing room conference with the judge or an appearance in the courtroom. Or, perhaps, they are hiding there—taking a break—trying to make it more difficult for court officers from other parts to locate them for their other cases.

"Good morning, Judge," they say to me in unison. The three sitting don't rise; the courthouse culture is that informal.

"Good morning. Hiding out, huh?"

I use the bathroom. When I leave, the lawyers are still there, chatting.

I return to my part. Angela and Bob are looking through the files on the desk in front of the bench. Two Legal Aid lawyers and an OLA lawyer are sitting in the back of the part.

"Elaine's conferencing two of the V's," Bob tells me.

"Good."

"I didn't hear any arms break in there," Bob says, referring to the plea conference from the last case.

"Nothing like that," I say. "I just made Gold's bones creak a little."

"I couldn't believe it," Bob shakes his head. "He had a terrible headache."

Angela looks up from the files and laughs.

I give them a fleeting look of resignation and cut it off, again walking the thin line between inappropriate judicial commentary and an overly formal distance. "Ah, well, life goes on," I say to them, and pause. "So what's up?"

"We got a bunch of things we can do," Bob says. "Jones is going to cover on the four extensions. Blaylock is on two of them and Roberts on another. One is a no-service. Schoffner's coming over from Part 4 and we can do an inquest with her and Blaylock. There's also a two-sider O withdrawal."

"They have lawyers?"

"No," Bob says.

"Well, let's go through the extensions and if Schoffner comes over, I'll hold her in here. I'll do the withdrawal after."

Angela fetches a Child Welfare Agency caseworker from the waiting area for the first extension. Jones, the OLA lawyer handling the four cases, and Blaylock, the Legal Aid lawyer on the first two, approach the counsel table.

"Extensions" is shorthand for extensions of foster care in child neglect and child abuse cases. A child may be "placed" with the New York City commissioner of Social Services for an initial period of up to one year once Family Court determines that a mother, father, or other person legally responsible for the child has neglected or abused the child. Before the end of the placement period, the commissioner may request court approval for foster care to be extended for up to another year. In theory, this process can continue without the child's consent until the child is eighteen.

"But we don't have Dan," Angela says now.

I should have known better than to let Dan out of the courtroom. "Well, he'll probably be back in a minute," I say, feeling inadequate somehow, as though the momentary breakdown of caseflow was my fault.

We sit for another minute or two, waiting for Dan. Annoyed at the delay, and with no one but myself to blame, I sit at the bench looking through my copy of New York's civil practice rules, trying to accomplish a quick piece of legal research. In the three-brother paternity case, I have been wondering why the lawyer for Brother #1 simply hasn't brought Brother #2 into the case as a third-party respondent. Reading the law, I appear nonchalant, but my anxiety over moving the calendar starts getting the better of me.

Dan returns. Bob calls the first of the extensions. The two lawyers stand and note their appearances. The caseworker is sworn in.

Extensions of foster care placement require a court hearing, with notice to the parent or other responsible person. As with most child protective cases, the New York City Legal Aid Society ordinarily represents the child as "law guardian." Many extension hearings are routine. Others raise complex issues regarding the quality of case services and planning on behalf of the foster child. Moreover, the extension petitions crowd the court calendars, "falling out of the ceiling all week," as the saying goes, making calendars already cluttered with new cases almost unmanageable.

Extension cases are important. In the most fundamental sense, they involve the essence of the Family Court's role in child protective cases: not simply to determine whether a child has been neglected or abused, but to play an active role in planning and securing the child's future—so-called permanency planning. Foster care is supposed to be a temporary solution. The desirable outcomes are successful reunification of the family, or adoption, or a grant of legal guardianship to a fit relative or other caretaker.

On the first of the four extensions this morning, I run into a problem. I've eyeballed the caseworker's one-page report that describes the current situation with these three children. The report tells me little, but it is clear that Mom has disappeared after a failed attempt at drug rehabilitation.

"I have an affidavit of service on the respondent mother, Your Honor," the OLA lawyer says, handing Angela a piece of paper to give to me.

I glance at it. Endorsing my sheet "A/S in file," I say, "The affidavit is made part of the record for purposes of the extension."

"We're recommending an extension of placement for one year, Your Honor," the OLA lawyer says then, following the approved script.

"What is the plan, if any, for terminating the mother's parental rights?" I ask the caseworker, who is standing next to the OLA lawyer. The caseworker is wearing a frayed gray tweed overcoat; he looks like a jazz musician at the end of an all-night gig.

"I don't know, Judge. I just got assigned this case. The other worker left the agency."

"Well, these children are with a maternal aunt, right?"

"Yes, Judge," OLA says, before the caseworker can say "I don't know" again.

"I don't see much point in continuing the foster care forever. The mother has dropped out of the picture. Is the aunt seeking to adopt the children?"

"I don't know, Judge," the caseworker says.

"Ms. Blaylock, would you like to inquire?" I ask the Legal Aid lawyer.

"Your Honor," Blaylock says, "I haven't been able to interview my clients and therefore I can't consent to the extension. I'd like an adjournment and I'd like to have the children produced for me to interview."

I take another look at the report. The children are eight, six, and three years old.

"Ms. Blaylock, you want to interview the two younger children? They're only six and three."

"I know, Judge, but I think I should see them."

"The mother is completely out of the picture here, Counselor," I say to her, keeping my tone level but calling her "Counselor" so that she will know I am irritated. "Even if you were to interview the children, what possible sensible course of action is indicated here other than extending foster care placement?"

"I don't know, Judge. I would like an adjournment to see my clients before consenting to the extension."

Feeling exhausted suddenly, I remind myself that the law guardian is absolutely right: What competent lawyer represents a client not yet even met?

"Fine, Ms. Blaylock. The application for the adjournment is denied. Placement is extended for a period of one year on all three children, the mother having defaulted following proper notice of this hearing. The mother is not available to care for these children. The agency is ordered to file a termination of parental rights petition versus the respondent mother and to report to the law guardian and the court within ninety days on the progress of that filing. The agency is ordered to produce the three children for the law guardian within ten days. Ms. Blaylock, after you see the children you may bring this case on the calendar for any appropriate purpose, for example if any unexpected problems involving the children are uncovered."

"Your Honor, I object," Ms. Blaylock says. "I—"

"Ms. Blaylock, your objection is noted, but I do not wish to hear any more argument on this matter. The caseworker may step out. Officer, call the next case, please."

"Your Honor, I—" Ms. Blaylock tries again before I cut her off again.

"We are off the record now on the last case, Ms. Blaylock."

Her face gets tight, but she stops. The caseworker hasn't moved an inch.

"Sir," I say to him. "You may step out now."

He gets a strange look on his face and the OLA lawyer says quickly, "Judge, he's the caseworker on the next one, too."

"Oh, excuse me," I say. "By all means, stay." And everyone chuckles, although there is bad air in the courtroom now.

Angela calls the next extension, which has the same cast of characters, nearly an identical set of facts except that there are two children instead of three, and, again, no respondent mother in the courtroom. We go through the script more easily this time; the law guardian has already interviewed the two children.

"Your Honor, we consent to this extension, but I would like to inquire of the caseworker."

"Go ahead, Ms. Blaylock."

"I understand from the children that they don't see each other very often. I realize they're in different foster homes, but why don't they have more visitation with each other?"

An acceptable question. The law encourages visitation among siblings.

"I don't know," the caseworker says. "This is also a new case for me. I just inherited it two weeks ago."

I interject immediately. "Thank you. Please report to the law guardian within two weeks with a response to her question. If the children aren't visiting with each other enough, please arrange for it to happen."

"Yes, Your Honor."

"Thank you, Your Honor," Ms. Blaylock says.

The caseworker leaves and Mr. Roberts replaces Ms. Blaylock at the Legal Aid end of the table. I do the no-service case first, extending placement temporarily and ordering personal service of the court papers on the mother for a hearing in thirty days.

Angela calls the next extension as I hand the previous endorsement sheet over to the clerk. Looking up, I see that the mother is present for this one. Her 18-B lawyer, a woman named Jones, stands next to her at the table. After the appearances are noted and the OLA lawyer has requested the one-year extension of placement, I nod at Jones.

"Your Honor," she says, "my client requests a hearing. She believes she is ready to have her son back and objects to the extension."

"Mr. Roberts, what is the law guardian's position on this? This is a seven-year-old, is that right?" I am shuffling through the papers as I speak, looking for the child's date of birth.

I am assuming the law guardian will argue in favor of the extension. The court papers say that the mother finished an outpatient drug program and a parenting course just one month ago. I look at the woman. As with most crack addicts trying only recently to stay clean, she's still too thin. But she's dressed OK and seems alert. Something about her gives me the impression she's intelligent. Yet, it may be too soon to return her son safely. But the law guardian surprises me.

"Your Honor, I've interviewed my client on this case. He is seven years old, as Your Honor said, and he is anxious to return to his mother. I recommend that placement not be extended and that the child be discharged to the mother under Child Welfare Agency supervision."

I stare at Roberts. The wish of a seven-year-old was controlling his argument. Then I tell myself to calm down, the man is just doing his job.

"Mr. Roberts, let me see if I understand your position here. You are comfortable with the court's returning a seven-year-old child to a woman who after several years of crack addiction has apparently stopped using drugs just recently?"

Jones struggles out of her chair and says, "Your Honor, I object to the characterization of—"

"Counsel, please approach," I tell them.

The three lawyers stand below me at the bench. I put my left palm up in the direction of the court stenographer to indicate we are going off the record. To Jones I say, "Listen to me, please. Your client seems like she's got a chance. Please don't expect me to blow it for her by returning this kid now. She'll never make it. You want to have a full hearing, fine, you're entitled to one. I'll extend placement temporarily and schedule a hearing date. But ask yourself how good your chances of winning are, even with Mr. Roberts on your side."

I look at the OLA lawyer and say, "Mr. Johnson, how about a six-month extension instead of a year? If the mother is still clean in ninety days, Ms. Jones, and you want to recalendar, you can do that."

"It's OK with me, Judge," the OLA lawyer agrees. "I'll ask the caseworker."

"Is this the actual caseworker for this family or just somebody covering?"

Johnson grins. "Yes, Judge, this time it is, in fact, the actual caseworker."

"Ms. Jones, will your client accept that?"

"Let me discuss it with her, Judge."

"Mr. Roberts?"

"Sounds reasonable, Your Honor."

"Thank you, Mr. Roberts. I try to be."

The lawyers return to their table to have the necessary discussions. While I am waiting, four more lawyers enter the courtroom, two 18-Bs, an OLA and a Legal Aid lawyer. Could my abuse trial be ready? No, they are the right 18-Bs, but the other two lawyers are here for a neglect inquest. Now the two 18-Bs whisper something to one another and leave the courtroom, no doubt headed for other cases. As they leave, Elaine, my law clerk, enters and gestures with the two "V" files to let me know she needs to talk with me about her case conferences. I indicate that I need about one minute.

"Counsel?"

"Your Honor," Ms. Jones says, "I have discussed with my client the settlement that was described at the bench conference and she will consent to a six-month extension."

Bingo. Another one disposed. OLA and Legal Aid also provide their assent for the record, I endorse the papers and read the endorsement into the record, and then everyone goes. I make a point of thanking Mr. Johnson as he leaves; he'd covered the four extensions and had shown up early in the day, helping to move the part calendar along. I was hoping that my little courtesies were going to bear fruit over the years.

Elaine starts towards the bench for our discussion, but I don't want to lose the two lawyers that have arrived for the neglect case. "Give me a minute, OK?" I say to her. "I want to get this inquest out of the way."

An inquest in a child protective proceeding—a trial in the absence of the parent or other caretaker—may proceed if the Child Welfare Agency proves that court papers were personally served on the parent or, with prior court authorization, served in some other manner reasonably calculated to give the parent notice of the proceeding. As with domestic violence cases, it is important, both tactically and in terms of basic fairness, for a judge to wait sufficiently long into the day to assure that, in fact, the person served is not going to appear. Doing an inquest too early runs the risk of a respondent appearing later in the morning. In that event, the case must nearly always be reopened, according to New York law in child protective cases.

What is adequate notice? How many chances should a respondent have to appear? How late should the court permit a respondent to be? No magic answers suggest themselves; the issue cuts both ways. On the one hand, the neglect or abuse of a child is serious stuff; the accused needs ample opportunity to defend against the charges. On the other hand, the very serious-ness of such accusations suggests that the accused would make every effort to appear in court and, moreover, to appear on time.

Deciding when to go forward with an inquest occasionally requires judicial self-discipline. There are days when the size of the calendar cries out for early action and the caseload fairly begs for relief. Yet, gradually, I was starting to veer more consistently in the direction of protecting the respondent's right to be present. As long as the children involved in a particular case were faring well, little was lost, on balance, from adjourn-ing a case for a few weeks—and especially if the notice given to a respondent seemed suspect.

Moreover, the information offered regarding a respondent's whereabouts wasn't always satisfactory. Here's an example from one of my cases:

OLA LAWYER: Your Honor, the matter is on for inquest. I am submitting an affidavit of service on the respondent mother. Service was made at the caretaker's address, the maternal aunt.

THE COURT: Well, there was no appearance of the mother on the last date when the case was called at 2:30. There is no appearance today at 10:45. Is the maternal aunt's address where the mother is living?

OLA: Uh, I'd have to ask the caseworker, Judge.

THE COURT: Let's do that. Sir, where is the mother living?

CWA CASEWORKER: I did not know her whereabouts until last Wednesday when I saw her at the aunt's home. She told me she is living in a shelter at [gives address].

THE COURT: How did you happen to find her at the aunt's house?

CASEWORKER: I just walked in on her. She was visiting the child.

THE COURT: Did you tell her about the court hearing scheduled for today?

CASEWORKER: I did not, no.

THE COURT: Why not?

CASEWORKER: I gave her an appointment to come to my office on Monday of this week. Apparently, that is when I thought I would be able to tell her. She didn't show up for the appointment.

THE COURT: Did you try to reach her at the shelter?

CASEWORKER: No.

THE COURT: The matter will be adjourned. Personal service is ordered on the respondent mother at the shelter.

And in another case:

OLA LAWYER: Your Honor, this is on for inquest. I am handing the court four affidavits of service.

THE COURT: Four?

OLA: Yes, Your Honor. We have tried a variety of addresses for personal service.

THE COURT (examining the affidavits): Do you want to try for the inside straight?

(Laughter in the courtroom.)

OLA: No, Judge. We'll stand pat.

THE COURT: Are any of these good addresses for the respondent?

OLA: I don't know, Your Honor.

THE COURT: I notice that service was not attempted at the maternal grandmother's house, which is where the children are living. Does the mother ever visit the children there?

CASEWORKER: Sometimes.

THE COURT: Do you think it might be useful to try service there?

CASEWORKER: I don't know, I—

OLA (interrupting): I get the point, Judge. We'll try service at the grandmother's.

Now, sitting at the bench, I take a quick look at the neglect allegations against the mother in this case. The case involves an "afterborn" child born "positive tox" to a crack addict. This means there is at least one prior neglect case against this mother and that the new baby tested positive for cocaine in his system at birth. In fact, this baby is the mother's third in a row to be born positive tox within five years. The mother is twenty-two years old.

The inquest involves, first of all, introducing into evidence the "2221" (Report of Suspected Child Abuse or Maltreatment) made by the hospital. New York's Social Services Law lists hospitals among the many mandated sources for such reports;

thus, the report can be introduced into evidence without anyone from the hospital in court.

Then, OLA elicits additional responses from the caseworker as to other allegations on the petition, such as the
mother's failure to try drug rehab, her abandonment of the
child, and prior neglect cases against her. This kind of inquest
ought to last no more than five minutes, and this one goes off
without a hitch.

I declare the child (who is called "Baby Boy," having no one
yet to name him), to be legally neglected, and proceed directly
to the end of the case, placing the child into foster care with the
New York City commissioner of social services. Why waste
another court appearance requiring the caseworker to do a
written investigation and report? The history and circumstances
here are quite clear. Mom is simply out of the picture; Dad was
never known. There are no relatives available for this child, so
he will be put in nonfamilial foster care as opposed to foster
care with relatives—so-called kinship foster care. A year from
now, I will no doubt see the case again, when it reaches the
court calendar for extension of placement. If the mother hasn't
surfaced, or if she has reappeared but hasn't begun rehabilitation, I will order the agency to file a case to terminate her
parental rights and free the child for adoption.

I leave the bench and go into the robing room to talk with
Elaine. A thirty-two-year-old lawyer with seven years of experience in Family Court, including several years as the managing
attorney of the Family Court division of a local legal aid society,
Elaine has been working as a law clerk in the New York City
Family Court for one year. The court's administrators quickly
recognized that she was one of their most knowledgeable and

practical lawyers. They had assigned her to me on a shared basis with Part 13. The arrangement wasn't going to last that much longer; a young lawyer named Barbara was taking the vacant full-time law clerk position. She had already started coming in for Elaine most afternoons.

Barbara was bright and energetic, with a sharp legal mind; Elaine, meanwhile, was mature beyond her years, had a great sense of humor, and was a terrific lawyer.

"Elaine, I always want you to talk candidly to me," I had said to her at the outset. "If you have a recommendation on a case or a legal issue, let it rip. If you think I'm heading in the wrong direction or that I made a mistake on a ruling, tell me. I'm going to do what I think is right anyway, but I want to hear from you."

On a daily basis, Elaine would split her time between Part 13 and Part 15, monitoring the progress of the calendar, discussing knotty cases in the robing room with me, giving opinions on legal and evidentiary issues that I flagged, and providing me with the benefit of her observations and experience. She was a whiz at conferencing domestic violence and child custody cases with litigants and lawyers in the waiting area, then bringing me proposed settlements to consider. Or she would advise me on another course of action in cases that couldn't or shouldn't be settled, needed additional inquiry from the bench, or required further probation department or Child Welfare Agency investigations or mental health studies.

"Good morning, Judge," Elaine says. "How's it going?"

"Not so terrible. I did the Mapp. Things are moving, but I have a lot."

"Sorry I was a little late."

"Nothing serious, I hope."

"No."

"Good."

"On the two V's, Judge, I've got one settled, I think, but I need to know how you want to handle it. The child is a seven-year-old boy. The mother is willing to give the father overnight visitation every other weekend, and that's OK with him, but no I & R was ever ordered."

The I & R reference is to an "investigation and report" that would be prepared by the New York City Probation Department regarding the two parents and their circumstances. Elaine continues, "They were never married, but he's legal Dad. Mom says he's OK."

"How did he seem to you?"

Elaine hesitates. She's cautious in her approach to these cases, a quality I like about her work.

"He seems sane enough, at least from the conversation I had with him, but you need an I&R," she says. "I'd only give him day visits until you get the report."

"Good. So that's one. What about the other case?"

"Well, they've both got private lawyers out there. And there's a law guardian for the kid. The kid's eight. I think you should order mental health studies on the parties and the kid should probably be seen, too. The father's lawyer says his client wants custody—the petition says custody—but I think it's really about visitation. A middle-class couple, they've been divorced for a year. The mother's lawyer says the kid doesn't want to see his father at all and that the father sexually abused the kid before the parents got divorced. I talked to the law guardian, Mr. Schroeder, and he says the kid told him his father used to sleep naked with him on visits when the parents were separated and there's some stuff about kissing the kid on the mouth."

"Are there any orders in the Supreme Court divorce decree?"

The Supreme Court is New York's general jurisdiction trial court and handles divorce cases.

"The Supreme Court referred the visitation issues to us, Judge. I don't think the father's had any visitation."

"All right, I'll take care of it. You know how long it takes to get a mental health study in a custody case now? Seventeen weeks."

"God."

"Yeah."

"Budget cuts. Thanks, Elaine. Listen, if the file isn't back upstairs already, can you grab the paternity case that was on this morning? I'd like you to take a look at the file."

In the courtroom, the two 18-Bs from the abuse case are talking to Bob. He comes over to the bench and says, "They want to know if you think we're going to get to their case before lunch."

I look at my watch.

"Yes. I want to do the two-sider O and the two V's first. We don't have OLA anyway, do we? Who's Legal Aid on the abuse case?"

"Ingelman. She checked in but I haven't seen her all morning."

What about Carr?" I ask, referring to an OLA lawyer.

"Carr is before the bench in Part 9." Angela says. "They say it'll be another twenty minutes."

"Well, tell the two of them to come back before noon. We can get it started, at least."

Bob consults with the two lawyers, then they leave. He says something to Angela. She goes out into the waiting area. When she opens the courtroom door, the noise from the waiting area surges in. It seems louder than a while ago, or perhaps I've been concentrating so hard I hadn't noticed it. In a moment Angela returns with a short woman and a huge guy who's got to be at least six feet, three inches tall.

As they enter, my clerk hands up a sheaf of orders to sign from the extensions of placement. I scribble my signature on the orders. Then, before Angela calls the domestic violence case, she says to me, "The woman told me she wants to drop the case, Judge."

"Your Honor, number 38 on the Part 15 calendar, in the matter of Thomas. Parties, raise your right hands, please."

Angela swears them in. I look at the woman and ask, "Are you still seeking an order of protection this morning, Ma'am?"

"No, Judge."

"You're not?"

"No."

"You're saying to the court that you want to drop this case?"

"Yes."

"Do you understand that the temporary order of protection that was issued to you will no longer be in effect once this case is withdrawn? That you will leave this courtroom without any order of protection against your husband?"

"Yes."

"Do any children live in the home?"

None are listed on the case papers, but I want to hear it from her.

"No."

"Well, ma'am, it's your case and obviously I can't force you to go forward. But I'm curious about something. You came to court saying this man tried to choke you and has in the past threatened you with a gun, right?"

She nods.

"Is this a gun that you actually saw?"

"No"

"Well, how close to blacking out did you get when he was choking you?"

"Well, I wasn't really blacking out."

"Now, this temporary order of protection I issued had excluded him from living in your home. That is what you asked for when you were here the other day. Did you have the police put him out?"

"No."

"You didn't?"

"No."

"May I ask why?"

"He has no place to go. I don't want him living on the street. I want to give him one more chance."

I say for the record, "On application of petitioner, the petition is withdrawn. Court staff shall refer the petitioner to the Victim Services Agency for services if petitioner desires."

Now I look over at her massive spouse.

"Sir, you've heard this woman say she's willing to give you another chance. I want you to know that if she brings another case against you in this court, that case will come before me. Now, nothing's been proved here about what you may or may not have done, but if anything similar ever is proved, I promise you, sir, it won't go well for you here."

"I didn't do nothing, Judge. We had an argument and she made this up."

"You may step out now." I point to the door.

"Step out, please," Angela says, but the guy doesn't move.

"Sir, step out of the courtroom, please," Bob says from behind him. The guy starts moving towards the door, glaring at me. He leaves, with the woman trailing behind him. I endorse the case papers: "On app. of pet., pet. W/D," and hand them to Ethel.

"Next," I say, sounding like a deli clerk. "But first I need a break."

I go out the side door, for the Part 18 robing room again, telling myself I really need to cut down on the coffee.

Fat chance.

From the robing room in Part 18, I can hear the judge yelling at a lawyer on the record.

"Mr. Young, I told you I had heard enough. Now stop your—"

"Judge, you're not giving me a chance to make a complete argument for the record. I want to say—"

"I said enough, Mr. Young. I'm warning—"

"Your Honor, that's not—"

"That's fifty dollars, Mr. Young. Contempt. Now stop talking."

"Judge, I—"

"Make it a hundred. What is the point of—"

"I strongly object to this treatment, Your Honor. I have a client. I'm just trying—"

"A hundred fifty. We can go as high as you like, Mr. Young. When I say stop, it means stop."

"I can't believe this, Judge. I—"

Listening, I shake my head. By the end of lunch hour, after a discussion in chambers between the judge and the lawyer, the contempt of court citation and the fine will be rescinded. I hadn't heard the entire exchange. Was the lawyer out of line?

Had the judge lost control? Whatever the provocation, it seemed likely to me, from the little I had overheard, that the judge hadn't built the careful, clear record for a contempt of court citation that would withstand an appeal: a record of prior unambiguous warnings from the bench, opportunities provided for the lawyer to apologize or regain composure, a final clear contempt warning, and only then the final blow. A contempt of court citation, sometimes casually administered in movie and television portrayals of courtroom drama, is in reality a drastic action only rarely applied. That particular rope has a lot of slack.

I get back to my part.

Bob says to me, "Judge, there's a lawyer out there on a B case who's driving me crazy. The father's been produced from prison, but the lawyer hasn't got service on the mother and wants an adjournment. The corrections guys want to start back upstate, too. You want to do it?"

"OK." Glancing at my copy of the day's calendar, I ask Bob, "Do we have Morrison?" referring to the father's court-appointed lawyer.

"He's right outside the part, Judge."

In one of the detention cells that serves Parts 15, 18, and 13 was a murderer doing twenty-five-years-to-life. A foster care agency had filed a case to terminate his parental rights with respect to his five-year-old son so that the foster parent could adopt him. These cases, called "TPRs" in Family Court, are assigned (I never figured out why) the letter-prefix "B" in the court's record-keeping system. In this case, the foster care agency alleged that the parents had abandoned the five-year-old child, who had been living with his foster parent for more than three years now.

Into the courtroom walks this six-foot, four-inch bear, flanked by two guards from the New York State Department of Corrections. In comparison, Morrison, the prisoner's short, thin lawyer standing next to him, looks as though he could be the guy's kid. Maybe we should file a case on Morrison, I say to myself, feeling giddy all of a sudden. Then I recognize the feeling: apprehension. Here is this murderer, this hulk, in my courtroom. Even with two court officers and two corrections officers in the courtroom, he seems menacing. And he was contesting the abandonment charges. Although today the child was safe and doing well in foster care, I felt responsible for his child's future.

Here was another test of Judge Ross's promise to himself: the less I liked someone who stood before me, or the less worthy a person's case seemed on the merits, the more carefully I would heed the relentless internal voice that told me when I was prejudging or cutting corners. First of all, I had my pride. And, I told myself, it was patriotic: I would offer due process of law to compete with the strip mall as one of my country's defining achievements. From my daily paces on the bench, I was beginning to glimpse—to sense, really, with imperfect comprehension—how elegant were our guarantees of due process and equal protection of the laws, although they sometimes played themselves out in less than elegant ways.

In other words, even this brute had rights.

Looking at him now, I pull myself together and handle the case.

"Your Honor," the foster care agency's lawyer says, "we're asking for an adjournment to complete service on the respondent mother."

"Needless to say, Judge, the father has no objection to the adjournment," Morrison pipes up, not that I'd asked him. Had Morrison's client been out of the courtroom, Morrison would have no doubt added, "My client has nothing but time on his hands, Judge," an oft-used tasteless line in prisoner cases.

As I am selecting an adjourned date, Angela walks behind the bench. I turn my swivel chair.

"What's up?"

"Judge," she whispers, "the corrections people don't want you to announce the next date in open court. They say it's for security reasons."

"What's that about?" I whisper back.

"I'm not sure. They said something about him making contact with people outside. Avoiding ambushes on the way to court, I don't know."

Everyone is looking at me. Angela moves away. I give the issue one second of thought, then decide: no way, he's entitled to know the date now, and besides, his lawyer is going to tell him.

I announce the next court date. The corrections officers exchange glances. Was I wrong? I wonder now. What do other judges do?

Dad is led away in handcuffs and Bob approaches the bench. "We've got three no-appearances, Judge," he tells me.

It's late enough in the morning to dismiss cases in which nobody has come to court. Today, two involve alleged domestic violence and one is about child visitation. Bob calls the cases and I say, "There is no appearance by any party, the petitions are dismissed." Glancing at one of them, I notice that it contains just one allegation: that the wife tried to poison the husband by putting Comet in his food.

All of the court parts had their famous domestic violence cases. In my part, for example, there was The Case of the Spirit Lady, in which the seventy-year-old sister of two brothers who lived in Atlanta sought orders of protection against their spirits, which were haunting her in the Bronx.

"They come to my bedroom window and tap at the window all night, Judge," she told me to the muffled laughter of the clerks, court officers, and lawyers observing in the courtroom.

"Well, ma'am, are you sure it's your brothers' spirits and not actual people? What floor do you live on?"

"The fourth."

"Is there a fire escape outside your bedroom window?"

"No."

"Well, what are these spirits wearing when they come?"

"One wears a plaid jacket. The other usually has just a shirt and pants."

I couldn't resist playing to the courtroom audience. "Ma'am, I can't violate either the letter or the spirit of the law in this case," I said to her, poker-faced. The muffled sound got louder. Suddenly, I felt ashamed. This sad old lady was staring at me, looking to me for help.

"Ma'am, I can only issue orders of protection against real people," I told her.

"Well, what do you suggest I do about them, Judge?"

A response popped into my head all at once as though deposited by a gremlin. Why not consult a spiritual advisor, ma'am? Or try wearing aluminum foil on your head to deflect the rays. The comment would have made me a courthouse hero for at least a week. Then I remembered an experienced judge's advice to me the first month I was on the bench: "Never forget,

Rick, these are real people you're talking to, no matter how wacky they might seem and no matter how hard it is to take the hundredth case of the day seriously. And you never know when a careless word might come back to haunt you."

"Ma'am, do you have a doctor?" I asked the woman now. "Someone that you see regularly and who knows you?"

"Well, yes."

"I'd like to suggest that you make an appointment right away. Tell the doctor what's been happening. I think that would help you a lot more than orders of protection, OK?"

"If you think that will help, Judge," she said.

"I think it would. Will you do that today?"

"Sure, Judge, if you say so."

"Thank you, ma'am. Please make the appointment today. The court officer will escort you outside the courtroom now."

I had The Case of the Evil Sisters, involving three siblings in their late twenties who occasionally beat one another bloody. They lived separately and sought protective orders against each other, for a total of six cases. All brought lawyers; nobody would consent to anything. I conducted one trial involving all of the latest alleged physical assaults and issued six orders of protection. Following the trial, and just prior to my issuing orders against his client, one of the lawyers tried some not-so-subtle coercion.

"My client is a production assistant with [naming a network evening news show], Your Honor," he told me in huffy tones. "The lies that have been told here today regarding her conduct and the court's acceptance of those as truth will not go unnoticed."

"Listen to me, please, Counselor," I said to her lawyer, "I don't care how many pencils your client sharpens for a living. I'm making my ruling and it's going to stand. If your client violates these orders of protection and it's proved to me that she did, she's going to jail. I suggest you make sure she understands." They all left as miserable as they came, but corralled by the force and limits of the orders of protection. Domestic violence cases, once the facts are proved, are about changing the balance of power in abusive relationships.

"Good one, Judge," the court officers told me. "I don't care how many pencils your client sharpens for a living. Love it."

"Let's bring in the V that Elaine settled," I tell Bob now.

"Judge, there's a return on a warrant on a hearing examiner case out there," Bob responds. "Can we do that first?"

"You have the file?"

"Yes. Here."

Looking over the papers in order to decide whether to call the case next, I find that I issued a warrant for a father in a child support case last month. A Family Court hearing examiner had found the father in "willful default" on a support order for his six-year-old son. Hearing Examiners are nonjudge lawyers who are appointed to hear and decide most child support cases in Family Court. New York law does not permit them, however, to jail parents who do not pay support. At that stage, the case is sent to a judge.

In this case, the child lived in Texas with his mother, who was on public assistance. Texas welfare authorities filed the case to recoup a portion of the public assistance payments made to the mother and forwarded the case to New York for processing because the father lived in the Bronx. Dad owed 200 weeks of child support payments at fifty dollars per week. In other words, $10,000. He hadn't made a payment—deliberately, the hearing examiner had determined—in nearly four years. This father was looking at a maximum of six months of incarceration.

"Get him 18-B and get the city's lawyer, the corporation counsel," I tell Bob. "I'll do it as soon as they're here."

"I already got them lined up. Is the guy going to go in?"

"I don't know."

Bob calls the case. Immediately, Dad's court-appointed lawyer starts pleading for mercy. Before he gets too far into the tale of hardship, I say to Dad, "Sir, it's already been determined that you willfully failed to pay ten thousand dollars of child support payments over the last four years. The question is how much money are you going to pay today?"

"I don't have any money, Judge," he says.

"Are you working, sir?"

"Yes."

"What do you do?"

"I'm a bartender."

We talk about his income, his current expenses, and his work hours.

"Judge, you can see he can't afford to pay the existing support order, much less come up with the arrears."

"You always have the option of filing to modify the order downwards, Counselor," I reply. "That's not the issue here. I'll tell you what, sir, you can pay the arrears back at the same rate you accumulated them, fifty dollars per week. And, of course, you still have to pay the original order as it accrues."

"But you're doubling my payment that way. It's hard to make expenses now, and I haven't got any money in the bank."

"Sir, you already told me that. What I'm saying is that—"

"And I only get to see him a couple of times a year. They've lived in Texas since he was a baby. It's not fair."

"Sir, that's not what you're standing in front of me about today. You owe the money, you've got to pay it."

Suddenly the city's assistant corporation counsel, who is prosecuting the case on the New York end, says, "Judge, we'd like him to pay a lump sum up-front, in addition to the extra fifty per week towards the arrears. This is a long-standing default. Four years."

The man groans. "I swear, Judge. I haven't got a dime."

"Judge—" his 18-B lawyer starts to say, but I cut him off.

"Look, folks, here's what's going to happen. Sir, my order on the arrears payment stands. And you're going to serve thirty days in jail, too, on fifteen consecutive weekends. You're working Monday through Friday, and I don't want you to lose your job. You'll receive instructions on how to report to jail, and if you don't go, sir, it will be reported to me and I'll be issuing another arrest warrant. That's all for now."

For fifteen weeks the guy's life will consist of work and jail. Any more jail time, I felt, would be so intolerable for him he might quit his job and disappear. The basic objective was to recover the money owed to the citizens of Texas who were supporting his son. I wanted Dad to keep his life intact. And also get the point.

Now we call the next case, the visitation case Elaine is supposed to have settled. When the couple walks into the courtroom, I can see that the woman is obviously angry.

"I understand that there has been a discussion in this case with my law clerk and that the two of you have reached an agreement in this case. Is that right, sir?"

He nods.

"I can't hear you, sir."

"Yes."

"Ma'am?"

"Yes." She looks annoyed.

"Let me tell you what I understand that agreement to be and if I am wrong about something, please let me know. Sir, you are to have visitation every other weekend, beginning this weekend, from Saturday morning at 11 A.M. to Sunday night at 6 P.M. and you are to pick up and deliver the child to the lobby of the mother's apartment building, where she will meet you. Is that your understanding, sir?"

"Yes."

"Ma'am?"

"Well, not exactly, Your Honor."

"What do you mean?"

"I don't want the visits to be at his apartment. They should be at his mother's house."

"You mean the child's grandmother?" I notice the guy is rolling his eyes and shaking his head.

"Yes."

"Why is that?"

"I don't want my son hanging around that new girlfriend."

Ah, the new girlfriend.

"Your Honor—"

"Not right this moment, please, sir." I hold up my hand. "Ma'am, these are overnight visits. Are you saying you want this man to live at his mother's house during the visitation weekend?"

"I don't care where he lives. As long as my son isn't around that woman."

"Well, now, ma'am, what's your problem with his girlfriend? Is it that you don't like her or do you believe she presents a danger to your son's life or health?"

She doesn't respond.

"Does she use drugs, ma'am? Or abuse your son? What's the problem?"

"Nothing."

"Sir, are you employed?"

"Yes."

"Where?"

"I work for the post office."

"Here in the Bronx?"

"Yes."

"How long have you worked for them?"

"Over three years now."

"I'll tell you folks what we're going to do. We've apparently got some conflict here. I think I want to find out a little more about you. I'm ordering a probation department investigation and report in this matter and I'm going to make a temporary order of visitation that will be good until the report is in my hands—that'll be about two months from now—and you come back to court. Sir, you may have visitation in the meantime every Saturday from 10 A.M. to 6 P.M. Ma'am, do you understand that's every Saturday, not every other weekend, but it's not overnight. Just Saturdays. Same pickup and delivery arrangement. Do you both understand?"

"The visits don't have to be at my mother's, Your Honor?" the man asks.

"That's right, they don't."

"Fine, Judge," he says.

"And you'll both be hearing from the probation department. Thank you. Court staff will tell you where to go for a copy of the temporary order."

"Parties step out, please," Bob says. They leave, the woman looking even more angry than when she walked into the part. "I don't think they're in love anymore, Judge," the court stenographer says.

I'm hoping the guy doesn't make remarks to her in the waiting area. She'll probably deck him. I'm also hoping he's the solid citizen he appears to be, but there's no point worrying about it now. Family Court judging: decide and move on.

Then, all at once, I realize I had forgotten to advise the parties that they had a right to a lawyer before I started to question them.

It's an imperfect world and you're an imperfect judge, I tell myself. I can advise them next time they are in court.

In come the two lawyers and the law guardian on the custody/visitation/sex abuse case that Elaine has conferenced.

"Your Honor, number 20 on the Part 15 calendar, in the matter of Vitello. Counsel, note your appearances, please."

I don't recognize the lawyers for Mom or Dad and I miss their names. Ex-husband and ex-wife are sworn in, then before the lawyers can speak I address myself to the child's law guardian. "Mr. Schroeder, you've interviewed the eight-year-old child in this matter, have you not?"

"Yes, Your Honor, I was able to interview him the last time the case was on."

Using my law clerk's information to move the case along, I ask, "And would you say that mental health studies are indicated on the parties and the child, based upon the results of that interview?"

"Well, Your Honor, I would. You know, all of us know that we hear a lot of things from parents and children in these kinds of cases and that it's not always advisable to take everything at face value, but I believe I heard enough from this child to recommend that the mental health study be done."

"Thank you, Mr. Schroeder. Now, Counsel, I'm going to order these studies, which will take three to four months to complete, based upon the law guardian's recommendation. Once the reports are in hand, we can proceed from there. And I don't think it would be useful this morning to get into the details of what may or may not lie behind the issues in this case."

"Well, Judge, are you going to make any temporary orders pending the studies?" Dad's lawyer asks. "Four months is a long time and my client isn't getting any cooperation from this woman with respect to visitation."

He says "this woman" as though she is dirt.

Immediately, Mom's lawyer says, "Judge, I object to the characterization of my client as uncooperative. There are serious sexual abuse issues here—"

"Those are being invented by your client and you know it," Dad's lawyer shoots back. "She's filling this child's head with the most unspeakable kind of—"

"Counsel, please," I interrupt. "I said I didn't think it was going to be useful to try to address the specifics this morning. Or is it afternoon already?" I look at my watch and make an expression of mock surprise. In moments of adversarial heat among counsel, I like to lean back in my swivel chair and speak in the softest of voices, taking on the manner of a bemused Grandpa.

The lawyers fall silent. "Your application regarding the temporary situation certainly needs to be considered," I say to Dad's lawyer, examining his client.

"Mr. Schroeder, what would be your recommendation in that regard?"

"Judge, I realize that four months is a long time, but until the mental health studies are done I don't think there should be any temporary orders, I'm afraid to say."

"Well," I say, "an underlying problem here is that this child doesn't seem to want to visit his father, whatever the reasons or the merits of them. Ordinarily, I might be prepared to consider a temporary order for a once-weekly, two-hour supervised visitation under the auspices of the Victim Services Agency here at the courthouse—that would be on Tuesday nights—but they only have a few slots and at least a three-month waiting list. Even then, the child is eight years old and might have his own ideas." Turning to the father's lawyer, I add, "Your client may be looking at a long period of trying to gradually regain the confidence of the child, if possible. I can't know that until I have the reports, but it's a reasonable working assumption at this point."

"Your Honor, I appreciate what you are saying, but I would still like you to make the temporary order for supervised visitation," Dad's lawyer says. He's applying the proper legal tactic of getting the precedent for visitation into the case if at all possible.

"No, I'm not going to do it at this point. Now let's pick an adjourned date and I'll order the studies. The clinic will be in touch with you."

So much for number 20 on the Part 15 calendar, in the matter of Vitello.

For today, that is.

Ah, custody cases. And oh, custody cases with sex abuse allegations. Increasingly, battles over child custody begin ordinarily enough, with papers served and the parties in court with lawyers, and temporary visitation orders made for the noncustodial parent, and a trial date set (hopefully, with a settlement to be reached on or before trial day). Then, several weeks later, Mom comes to court to end the visits. Dad is a pedophile, she says. She has learned from her little girl (or little boy) that Dad has been sexually abusing the child for weeks, months, even years. The child has begun to have nightmares or stomachaches, or seems depressed after school, or cries following visits with Dad. The mother has taken the child to a doctor, or therapist, where the child has said that Daddy has been doing x, y, z, or worse to her since God knows when.

And visitation ends. A court-ordered investigation follows, conducted by the Child Welfare Agency and which includes, perhaps, a series of interviews with the child by a mental health professional. Dad denies everything. His lawyer, outraged, shouts "foul," yells for Mom's scalp, and demands that Dad's own expert examine the child next.

From a judge's viewpoint, certain accusations seem immediately suspicious, a feeling based on Mom's demeanor, or on evidence of previous, unfounded sex abuse allegations made by her against Dad, or on an absence of corroborating medical evidence or convincing professional psychological support for the charges. Nevertheless, no Family Court judge acts on initial instincts in these kinds of cases. The risk to the child is too great. Quickly, every judge discovers that you can never have enough information on the bench; caution is the watchword; surprises are not infrequent; too often, experts disagree, or information turns out to be incomplete or just plain wrong. Of course, at some point you have to go with what you have; knowing when to decide is as important a part of the craft of judging as making the right decision.

Meanwhile, the child suffers. It goes without saying that the more serious victims are those who have actually been abused. The damage to these children is horrible, unimaginable. Yet, the process of investigation, and the separation of the child from the accused parent, leave nasty scars on the children involved in false allegations.

I was on the bench for nearly one year when the Woody Allen/Mia Farrow case hit the media. Such notoriety! My colleagues and I were each handling dozens of such cases, more than a few with allegations at least as shocking and family lives more tortured than those involving the children of these two celebrities. Not to diminish the obvious misery involved in their case, but where was the spotlight on the common folk of Brooklyn, Queens, Manhattan, the Bronx, and Staten Island, too? Watching the news clips, I would say to myself, bring on the Woody Allen case. I'll show them how we Family Court judges have to do it. In the middle of the morning, after our fourteenth, fifteenth, or twentieth case, one turns to the court officer and says, "What's next? The Woody Allen case? OK, let's get them in here. And line up the next three cases, would you?"

In fact, child custody cases can raise any number of difficulties. The Case of the Left-For-Dead Mother had me yearning for the skills of a miracle-worker. While living in Vermont five years ago, Dad had stabbed Mom a dozen or so times, dumping her in the Green Mountains where a dog sniffed her out two days later. She was barely alive but survived to prosecute her husband, who is now serving twenty years in a Vermont state prison. Their daughter was eighteen months old at the time of the stabbing. Packed up by Dad's mother, sister, and brother to live with them in the Bronx, the girl knew nothing of the murder attempt. Dad was in prison for robbery, she was told, and Mom had deserted the family. The girl visited with Dad every other month. Six years and several rounds of surgery and rehab later, Mom found her daughter with the assistance of a private investigator. She wanted visitation. If the relationship developed satisfactorily, she wanted custody.

But her daughter, now nearly eight, wanted no part of any of it, according to the lawyer I appointed for the girl. She believed her mother had abandoned her. Her lawyer had so far told her nothing of what took place in Vermont.

"Judge, I think we can get a book contract out of this one," the girl's lawyer joked just before the case was called one day. "Or at least get on *Prime Time Live*."

"No, thank you," I told her, unamused. "Just see if you can figure out what to do."

It seemed outrageous to me that the father's relatives had hidden the girl from her mother, no doubt to prevent the truth from reaching the child. Yet, as the evidence developed over several court appearances, I became convinced (although their deception was sticking in my craw, to say the least) that the relatives were in all other respects good caretakers and that, so far, the little girl was normal and content. Nevertheless, as the natural parent, the mother had the legal right to her daughter's custody, unless they could offer proof that Mom was unfit or had abandoned the child. So far, no such proof was forthcoming; in fact, the mother was the victim of an awful assault and a monstrous deception. Still, I could not avoid considering whether it was in her daughter's best interests at this time to visit, much less return to Mom. In all likelihood, the truth would emerge during the visits. Would that truth devastate the girl? Was there a way to protect and promote the girl's well-being while encouraging the development of the mother-daughter relationship?

Eventually, I made two orders: "Reasonable visitation for the mother as the child desires" and "The present custodians are to arrange for a course of counseling the child regarding her mother's re-appearance; until otherwise ordered by the court, any such visits to take place at the office of, and under the supervision of, a therapist." Everyone left the courtroom that day unhappy.

The Case of the Clinging Boy was another strange one. A six-year-old was refusing to visit with his father following several years of regular alternate-weekend visitation. Moreover, I was being told by the child's lawyer that the boy would barely talk to anyone except his mother. Ordinarily, young children are left in the courthouse nursery, or with a relative in the waiting area, while their parents are in the courtroom. This child, however, would start screaming when a separation was attempted. The mother walked into my courtroom with the boy in her arms, his face buried in her chest, his hands clasped, white-knuckled, around her neck. He was small, but she struggled under his weight.

"Judge," the boy's lawyer said to me, "I can't even get the child to talk to me, and I like to think I have a fair amount of experience interviewing children. I strongly suggest you try to have an in camera interview with the child. Maybe you'll have better luck."

An "in camera" interview referred, at minimum, to an inquiry outside of the courtroom. With any luck, the child would feel less threatened in a smaller room and by a somewhat less formal procedure. I looked at the lawyers for Mom and Dad. "Well, Counsel, I'm prepared to do that in the robing room right now. This would be on the record, but without anyone present besides me, the court stenographer, the child, and the boy's lawyer."

The father's lawyer shrugged. The mother's lawyer said, "Your Honor, I don't think you're going to be able to get the child to go into the robing room without his mother."

"In that case, Judge," the father's lawyer spoke up, "my client wants to be there, too."

Making a quick judgment, I said, "Counsel, listen to me, please. I'd prefer not to have either parent there. But if it's necessary to have the mother in the room I will permit it. However, she will not be permitted to participate in the interview."

"I object, Your Honor," the father's lawyer said. "At least I should be permitted to be present, too, if the father can't be there and the mother can."

"If he can be there then I should be allowed as well, Your Honor," the mother's lawyer said.

"There would be too many people in the robing room at that point," I replied. "It would overwhelm the child and likely defeat the purpose of the procedure. Your objection is noted for the record, Counsel, and of course you would have the opportunity to review the transcript of the in camera interview if you are concerned that your client's rights have been prejudiced in some way."

In the robing room I hung up my robe. The court stenographer began to get her gear together. The mother and the boy and the child's lawyer joined me. I sat at the robing room desk, rolling up my shirt sleeves, trying to make things more informal for the little boy. When the court stenographer was ready, I moved my chair alongside the desk and leaned towards the child, who was still clinging to his mother, his back to me.

"Hello, Timmy," I said, trying to get him to at least look at me in profile.

Nothing.

"Do you know who I am, Timmy? My name is Judge Ross. I'd like to talk to you for a minute, OK?"

No, it wasn't.

"Well, Timmy, I know this might be a little scary for you, but do you think you could try to talk to me? How would you like to sit in my chair? I'll move over to where you are."

Silence.

The kid's lawyer said to the mother, "Ms. Johnson, do you think you could try to get Timmy to let go of you for a minute? Maybe he could sit on your lap facing the judge."

The mother looked embarrassed. "I'll try."

She reached up and tried to unclasp Timmy's hands. He grabbed tighter.

"Timmy," she said, "you're hurting Mommy. Would you like to let go and talk to the judge?"

I'd seen enough.

"Listen, folks, this is only frightening the child. Let's go back in the courtroom."

They walked out of the robing room. As she left, Timmy's lawyer looked over her shoulder and said, "You see what I mean, Judge?"

Alone in the robing room for a minute, I considered the next move. What was going on here? Any visitation order would be meaningless—unenforceable—and it wasn't as though the mother was actively preventing visitation. In fact, she didn't seem to have a clue about the cause of her son's behavior. I wondered how they even got this child to go to school.

Then, from nowhere, I had a clear thought: Sexual abuse. Nobody had mentioned it, and I certainly didn't want to borrow trouble, but there it was flashing in bold colors in my head.

I put on my robe and went back into the courtroom. "All rise, come to order," Bob said as I entered.

"Please be seated," I told everyone. "What I'm going to do in this case is to order the court's mental health clinic to interview the parties and the child and I would like the clinic's assessment of the child to include an evaluation of possible pathology related to interaction between the child and any adults with whom he might have been having regular contact, including the father on the visits that have been occurring over the last several years. I'm not suggesting that there is any such pathology or that anything untoward has occurred, but let's not be coy. This child is scared stiff of something, and it would be irresponsible not to try to determine what it is."

I waited for the protest from the father. The child's lawyer was nodding her head and giving me an approving look.

No one said anything, so I continued, "I'm going to ask the clerk to call the clinic and get a sense of what their earliest appointment might be. The matter will be recalled in ten minutes and we'll pick an adjourned date once I have that information."

I moved on to another case. Soon, Ethel came out of the robing room and got my attention. I beckoned her over.

"I talked to the clinic, Judge," she whispered to me. "They're not taking any more referrals in custody or visitation cases for four months."

"What?"

"That's what they said."

I finished the case that was before me and went into the robing room. I called the clinic and asked for the director. When she got on the phone, I said, "Ms. Smoller, this is Judge Ross. Someone just told my clerk you weren't taking referrals for four months in visitation cases."

"I said that."

"What's the deal? I've got an emergency."

"We're short-staffed, Judge, just like everyone else. There are just no appointments."

"What are you doing for emergencies?"

"You mean to send someone to the hospital?"

"No."

"Well, that's how we define an emergency."

"Well, this case is an emergency. I need a six-year-old boy evaluated for sexual or physical abuse. Preferably within the next two weeks. I'd certainly appreciate your cooperation."

"Well, Judge, I—"

"I'll put the case on the calendar for three weeks from today. That should give you time to prepare a written report as well."

"Judge, it's just not—"

"Ms. Smoller, please. I have to get back on the bench. I'm going to prepare a short order directing you to do this. The clerk will bring it to you with the case file."

There was a pregnant pause.

"All right, Judge, I'll do it for you." (Ah, a personal favor, the old face-saver.) "I hope you can appreciate that."

"I certainly can," I cut her off. "And it is appreciated. Thank you. The clerk will bring you the order and the file." (A reminder: an order, not a favor.)

I recalled the visitation case, set an adjourned date, and went on to the fifteen other cases left on the calendar that day. Several months later, I had the opportunity to read the criminal indictment against Dad for sodomizing Timmy over a period of nearly a year.

Or consider The Case of the Lesbian Softball Team. This was a custody proceeding in which a man recently separated from his wife sought to rescue (as he put it) their two teenage children from the "illicit lifestyle" adopted by his wife. Armed with neighborhood rumors, Dad summoned welfare authorities and the police to accompany him to his wife's new apartment where, he told them, they would now find her living—with eight other women! The children must be removed at once!

In fact, on that particular afternoon there they were, all nine of them, his (soon to be ex-) wife, and the shortstop, and the catcher, and the center fielder, and the designated hitter, and the rest of the members of the team; plus the bats, and the balls, and the gloves, too. Lesbians, to be sure, but what of it? Was there a law against forming a team and playing in a local softball league? As the team members left the scene and headed for home, only his wife and the left fielder—her new partner— remained. The police and welfare authorities left.

His next stop: Family Court.

Yet, as I sorted out the facts, I began to become concerned, though not on the grounds of the woman's sexual preference. The new partner had two kids of her own, six and eight years old. It seemed to me that the living space in the apartment was inadequate and the sleeping arrangements inappropriate. The place was one bedroom short for two adults and four children. The two kids at the heart of the case were thirteen-year-old and fifteen-year-old girls; it sounded to me, though Mom changed the details under my questioning, that she and the teenagers might be sleeping in the same bed. I ordered a welfare investigation, appointed a lawyer for the children, and ordered Mom to bring the children to court on the next date. Dad left the courtroom looking smug, but without custody.

Things turned out OK when the case came back. The welfare investigator reported that the children were in good health, attending school, and eating well. The lawyer I had appointed interviewed them. They told her that Mom and her partner took good care of them and that they liked living in the new setup. They didn't sleep with Mom (they claimed), but in their own bedroom in twin beds. Something about this aspect of the case was bothering me. I ordered Mom to move to the sofa bed in the living room with her partner. The two bedrooms must go to the children.

"This is a condition of your having custody," I told Mom.

I expected her to complain, but she agreed readily, without even consulting her partner.

We worked out a twice-weekly visitation arrangement for Dad. The lawyer for the children reported that they had complained to her about Dad's conduct during visits. He pestered them with questions about Mom and what went on in the house. They hated it.

"Sir, if you can't keep your feelings toward your wife out of your relationship with your children, it's not going to continue to be in their best interests to visit with you," I told him. "And they don't need me for that, they're old enough to make their own decisions. They're going to stop coming over if you're not more considerate of their feelings, sir."

They left, she with an order of custody, he with an order of visitation. Case closed, for now.

"Thank you, Your Honor," Dad said to me as he walked out of the courtroom.

I didn't reply. He came to me for custody and left with only visitation and a warning.

Every day held new surprises. Neutrons would decay before the case variations ended.

Now Bob walks over to the bench. "You going to do the abuse case in the robing room with just the lawyers, Judge? They're going to bring the kid around the back. Everybody's ready."

"No, the robing room's too small. Let's do it around the counsel table. I'll sit with everybody."

In this child abuse case filed by the New York City Child Welfare Agency, I had to take the testimony of an eight-year-old girl whose out-of-court (hearsay) description to a school psychologist of sexual abuse at the hands of her grandfather could not be corroborated by any other evidence and thus would have been inadmissible at the trial. The lawyers for the grandfather and the mother (who was charged with failing to protect the girl from live-in Grandpa) had agreed to the exclusion of their clients from the courtroom during the child's testimony. In most Family Court child neglect or child abuse cases, the child doesn't testify; the accused parents or other accused caretakers are present in the courtroom during the trial.

Sitting at the table with me are the Office of Legal Affairs lawyer, the respondents' lawyers, the child, the child's law guardian, and the court stenographer with his machine. The child's Legal Aid Society lawyer, a woman who seems to have established a comfortable relationship with the little girl, explains to her what is going on and who we all are. Quickly we resolve several legal issues, then with those disposed of, the child's law guardian conducts the direct examination of the girl. (A bit of it follows; I'll skip the painful cross-examination.)

LAW GUARDIAN: Brenda, do you know the difference between a good touch and a bad touch?

CHILD: Yes.

LAW GUARDIAN: Can you tell me what a good touch would be?

CHILD: If I gave my grandpa—I mean if he gave me a hug, that would be a good touch.

LAW GUARDIAN: And what would be a bad touch?

CHILD: Somebody touched my private parts.

LAW GUARDIAN: OK. And what are your private parts?

CHILD: My vagina.

LAW GUARDIAN: OK. And did anybody ever touch you in your private parts?

CHILD: Yes.

LAW GUARDIAN: Who was that?

CHILD: My grandpa.

LAW GUARDIAN: Do you remember when he did that?

CHILD: When I—yes, when I was living with him one summer.

LAW GUARDIAN: Can you tell me exactly how he touched you?

CHILD: With his finger.

LAW GUARDIAN: OK, and where did he touch you at?

CHILD: In my private parts, my vagina.

LAW GUARDIAN: Did he do anything else?

CHILD: Yes. He showed me nasty magazines and nasty tapes.

LAW GUARDIAN: And when you say nasty, what do you mean by nasty?

CHILD: People who don't have clothes on.

LAW GUARDIAN: When your grandpa touched you, do you remember what grade you were in?

CHILD: I think I was in second grade.

LAW GUARDIAN: OK. Why don't you tell us what your grandpa did to you?

CHILD: He made me touch his penis.

LAW GUARDIAN: Yes, and what happened?

CHILD: And he made stuff come out of it in the bathroom.

LAW GUARDIAN: What is a penis?

CHILD: That is a man's private.

LAW GUARDIAN: You said something about stuff coming out of a penis, what kind of stuff, do you remember?

CHILD: (Nods.)

LAW GUARDIAN: What did it look like?

CHILD: It is white stuff. My grandpa said it was babies.

LAW GUARDIAN: Did you talk to your mom about this?

CHILD: I told her.

LAW GUARDIAN: And what did she say?

CHILD: She talked to my grandpa about it.

LAW GUARDIAN: Oh, and after that, did you talk to your grandpa?

CHILD: Yes.

LAW GUARDIAN: And what did your grandpa say to you?

CHILD: He said he promised he wouldn't do it again.

LAW GUARDIAN: OK. And did he do it again after that?
CHILD: Yes.
LAW GUARDIAN: How many times?
CHILD: A couple of times.

Awful, but unfortunately, fairly standard testimony. Brenda would stay in foster care and undergo several years of psychotherapy before returning home after Grandpa died.

A half-dozen of these child abuse trials into the job, while listening one afternoon to a Child Welfare Agency caseworker relate a ten-year-old girl's description of being molested by her stepfather, I realized that I couldn't recall what the stepfather looked like. Yet he had been sitting at a table not more than twenty feet away, facing me, for nearly an hour. It occurred to me that in all likelihood I could provide only the vaguest description of the men involved in the child abuse cases over which I had been presiding. In no other type of case was this true. As with all Family Court judges, it was usually automatic for me to scrutinize everyone who came into my courtroom.

I understood at once. Don't look, none of this is real: neither flesh nor blood, nor hot drunken breath, nor stubble of beard, nor smell of sweat, nor rub of skin. Just words in the air.

Scary monsters.

Often, the first thing judges from other courts would say to me, upon learning that I sat in Family Court, was, "I don't see how you hear those cases. I'd jump over the bench and strangle those bastards. I just couldn't sit there and listen."

I began to study these men, the dads and stepdads and grandpas and boyfriends of Mom ("paramours," in Family Court jargon), and the moms, too, including the moms charged with letting the abuse continue once they learned of it. A common characteristic became apparent: the absence of emotion in their faces and in their body language as they heard the excruciating details of the suffering of their children and wards. J'accuse, the children, and lawyers, and caseworkers, and physicians, and psychologists, and social workers, and guidance counselors, and teachers would say to them from the witness chair, and they would sit, unmoving, their stares and postures yielding no clue.

Soon, I learned just to look them over and then ignore them. They weren't, after all, what my cases were about. Let the Criminal Term justices deal with the perps. Family Court was about the children. New York's child protective law puts it this way: "This article is designed to establish procedures to help protect children from injury or mistreatment and to help safeguard their physical, mental, and emotional well-being. It is designed to provide a due process of law for determining when the state, through its family court, may intervene against the wishes of a parent on behalf of a child so that his needs are properly met."

The caselaw growing out of this statute is unambiguous: safeguarding the well-being of the children is the Family Court's primary function in child protective cases. As long as the accused are represented by counsel, and the rules of evidence are correctly applied at trial, and the facts are proved by the required standard of proof ("a preponderance of the evidence"), and the proof spells out the legal definition of abuse or neglect—why, then, I can proceed to protect the child over the long haul. The interests and needs of the moms, dads, and other caretakers are secondary.

But not really. Any judge with a notion of keeping children at home in appropriate cases had to be sure that the parents' needs—for example, psychotherapy, parenting skills training, treatment for drug addiction, or homemaker assistance, among other possibilities—are being successfully addressed. The legal issue for a New York City Family Court judge during a child protective case is whether keeping a child at home with an allegedly neglectful or abusive parent or other caretaker presents an "imminent risk to the child's life or health." If not, the law requires that the child stay at home during the case. When the Child Welfare Agency has removed a child from home on an emergency basis, or a Family Court judge has ordered the child removed, the same law that contains the "imminent risk" language also provides parents with the right to a hearing, within three days of the removal, if they want the child to return home. These hearings, called "1028" hearings for the Family Court Act section that mandates them, are often more hotly contested than the trial that determines whether the children are to be considered legally neglected or abused.

Call me abusive, call me neglectful, but just don't take my kids away. . . .

The responsibility to safeguard children comes with the judicial turf. Sometimes it is necessary to act even when a child protective caseworker advises otherwise.

OLA LAWYER: Your Honor, the commissioner is asking for a parole [release] for this child [an eight-year-old boy].
THE COURT: Parole to the respondent mother?
CHILD WELFARE AGENCY CASEWORKER: Yes. The child is with the mother at home now.
THE COURT: What is the basis for the recommendation? I'm reading the allegations you've filed against her. You're saying

she uses crack and won't go into treatment. This is the second child she has had while using cocaine.

CASEWORKER: The mother has a good support system. The home is adequately furnished. There's food in the home and the child attends school. In terms of the child's health and safety, the child is well cared for. There is a grandmother; although she does not live in the home, she makes daily visits.

THE COURT: The child is well cared for and should stay at home, despite the fact that you're filing a neglect petition against the mother on the basis that she hasn't cooperated with drug rehabilitation and is a crack user?

CASEWORKER: Yes.

THE COURT: What's the logic there?

CASEWORKER: Well, Your Honor, I feel the child is well cared for in the home.

THE COURT: Wouldn't the child be better off with the grand-mother?

CASEWORKER: The grandmother has other children. She has no room for this child.

THE COURT: Is there a father in the picture?

CASEWORKER: No.

THE COURT: Would the law guardian like to inquire of the caseworker?

LAW GUARDIAN: Yes, Judge. Is the child attending school?

CASEWORKER: Yes.

LAW GUARDIAN: What is the child's date of birth?

THE COURT: It's on the petition, Counselor. Do you have questions more closely related to the care of the child?

LAW GUARDIAN: No, Judge. I'd like the child produced for me to interview on the next court date.

THE COURT: When was the last time the mother used crack?

CASEWORKER: Last month, Judge.

THE COURT: I'm not releasing the child to a crack user who refuses rehabilitation, regarding whom a neglect case has now been filed, whether or not everyone says she's taking good care of the child. The imminent risk seems obvious to me. The child is remanded to the commissioner of social services [placed in foster care].

Getting to know the different caseworkers helped, although staff turnover and transfers made it difficult to become familiar with as many caseworkers as I would have liked. As I began to relax a bit in the job, I was able to permit myself to visualize what my child removal orders meant: one, two, or more caseworkers, accompanied by the police, gathering up the belongings of a crying (screaming?) child and taking the child from home, parent(s), and, perhaps, brothers and sisters. From there, if no suitable relatives were immediately available, a trip to "allocations," the foster care holding unit where children and nonkinship foster homes are matched, and then to a stranger's home. I started to ask myself, are the fact patterns upon which I was removing children truly presenting imminent—"about to occur, impending"—risk to their lives and health? Was I permitting state intervention too casually?

Yet, to release a child to a caretaker who is using drugs, or to a home where domestic violence has occurred or a child has been beaten—such a decision raised issues of enormous consequence to the child. Could I rely on the caseworker to supervise the family closely and safeguard the child at home? Would I obtain accurate information about the child's care? Was the judgment of the child's law guardian sound? With experience, I learned that the answer to these questions was: not always. And one can't simply take a leap of faith when the safety of a child is involved.

Many of the removal decisions were no-brainers. Others seemed obvious but for some reason gave me pause. One of my first 1028 hearings involved foster parents who had cared for more than twenty children, including two children they had adopted and their three biological children. At the time of the 1028 hearing they had eight children in their home: their own five, two young foster children, and a baby who was the son of their adult daughter still living at home.

Their four-year-old adopted daughter suffered from cerebral palsy. In November, during a physical examination at a hospital clinic, a nurse noticed healing loop-shaped scars on the child's back, upper arm, thighs, and buttocks. Six months earlier, at a regularly scheduled physical, no marks were evident. Doctors from the hospital's child abuse team characterized the marks as "cord marks consistent with child abuse." Once notified, the Child Welfare Agency placed the child in a foster home and filed a neglect petition against the parents, citing the inadequacy of their explanation of the injuries.

In fact, Dad was offering no explanation at all, claiming not even to have known the marks existed. Mom admitted to having seen the marks for the first time two weeks prior to November's physical exam. She attributed them to an accident on a swing which she claimed her adult daughter had reported to her when she and Dad returned from a visit to North Carolina in mid-October, having left the children in the daughter's care. According to the doctors, however, the characteristics of the scars were inconsistent with Mom's explanation.

The Child Welfare Agency had not removed any of the other children. In fact, the neglect case named only the two adopted children—the scarred four-year-old and her six-year-old brother—as having been neglected. According to the agency and the children's law guardian, no injuries or imminent risk to the life or health of the six-year-old existed; he should stay at home. Nor was the agency prepared to seek findings of neglect with respect to the other children.

Hiring lawyers, the parents requested a 1028 hearing to have their adopted daughter returned.

The hearing took half of two days and an hour of a third. Meanwhile, during breaks in the hearing, I was doing the rest of my calendar at warp speed; since 1028 hearings can't be anticipated, I had a full calendar already scheduled for those days. The lawyers for Mom and Dad probed every witness and every piece of documentary evidence with thoroughness. Even better, they had a theory of defense. They tried to make the swing accident seem plausible. In addition, they were discovering the agency's case, drawing out the evidence for the main trial.

At the end of the hearing, I felt certain of at least one decision. In the absence of a credible explanation for the child's injuries, Mom and Dad couldn't be trusted with the little girl. And because they would admit to no fault in their conduct or attitudes, it was not possible to fashion a service plan for the family that would promote the safety of the child at home. Nor could one or the other parent be removed from the home under a protective order so that the child could be safely returned. I had no way to know which parent to exclude.

This much was straightforward. But what of the other children? Were they in danger? Or was I seeing a not uncommon case of abuse of a special needs child, in which only the child most difficult to handle or control is abused by the parents? There was no evidence of direct abuse or neglect of the other children. The agency and law guardian claimed there wasn't any. Nevertheless, a parent who caused this little girl's injuries was capable of anything, right? Should I order, at minimum, her six-year-old brother removed? Nobody was asking me to. Imagine that child's shock and confusion as the police and caseworkers packed his clothes and took him away, this orphan who had been rescued—it was true, was it not?—by these two strangers who had adopted him.

When the hearing ended, I talked things over with my law clerk in chambers at lunch hour. A decision was due after lunch.

"It would be perfectly appropriate to remove the other kid, Judge," she said to me. "You wouldn't be out of bounds."

"I know. It seems obvious. So why is the law guardian so insistent otherwise?"

"Well, if you're wrong, you'd be erring on the safe side."

"I'm going across the street to get a bagel," I said to her. "You want anything?"

"No. I'll come down to the part after lunch."

Outside, in the chill, I thought about it. The law guardian wanted the other child to stay at home. Obviously, she believed the six-year-old would be safe.

Waiting on line in the bodega, I got myself back to judicial basics, the evidence. The scars on the six-year-old's younger sister were ugly; the pictures the agency had introduced into evidence were extremely disturbing. What more did I need? I couldn't trust these parents. Never mind the impending traumatic scene when the injured girl's brother is taken from home. I was letting sentimentality overcome the logic emerging from the hearing evidence. Reading the papers in 1995 and 1996 shocked even the most jaded New Yorkers: one child's death followed another amidst gruesome accounts of seemingly endless child abuse. New York City Family Court judges have a saying—"any day, any case"—that reminds us how important it is to maintain focus and keep concentrating.

The six-year-old went into foster care.

Both inside and out of the child protective system, "family preservation" is a significant social objective that is reflected in service agency policies and procedures. Some denounce this objective as too frequently ignoring the safety of children. But what rational person doesn't favor, in theory, the preservation of families? Yet, if a child's home presents imminent risk to the child's life or health while a child protective case is pending, and if I am not convinced that parental support services or other measures will safeguard the child, I am going to take the child out of the home. The law requires it: end of story.

One of the more charged issues in the social services debates is kinship foster care. In 1996, approximately one-third of the nearly 43,000 children in foster care in New York City were in the care of relatives—so-called kinship foster parents.

These relatives receive "Eugene F." funds, named for the 1986 case of *Eugene F. v. Gross*. That case resulted in enforcement of the principle, already established in the law, that New York City children placed in foster care with relatives are entitled to the same amount of financial support as children in the foster homes of unrelated caretakers.

In 1986, few if any expected that during the next ten years the number of New York City children in foster care would more than triple, and that children in the care of relatives would increase sixfold. Eventually, the cost of this care rose to nearly one billion dollars annually, much of it coming directly from the pockets of New York City taxpayers, with New York State and federal taxpayers supplying the rest. If you were a grandma or aunt caring for your grandchildren, nieces, or nephews as kinship foster children, your monthly payment would be between $400 and $600 for each child, depending on the child's age. Compare this with the $100 per month of ordinary welfare payments (AFDC payments, for Aid to Families with Dependent Children) that would be available if you simply took legal custody of your daughter's or sister's children outside of the foster care system. Not to mention the additional foster care diaper and clothing allowances, as well as taxpayer-supported medical benefits and other services.

Some people seethed over this level of tax-free payment to relatives. As one woman put it at a public forum I attended several years ago, "Family members shouldn't be paid for what they are morally obligated to do to begin with." Occasionally Aunt somebody-or-other would surface in a courtroom with a monthly payment of $3,000-$4,000 for taking care of five or more of these children. Every now and then the courthouse would buzz with a story of one caseworker or another handing over a retroactive Eugene F. payment to a relative in the form of a tax-free check for $20,000, $30,000, or more. It made some people want to quit work, or so they said, shaking their heads and gritting their teeth.

Yet, it seemed to me that the answer to objections to kinship foster care funding—which, after all, was approved by law—lay also in the law. The majority of New York City children in foster care have been there for more than two years, although foster care, kinship or nonkinship, is intended as a temporary solution. The New York statutes and caselaw make that clear. New York City's commissioner of social services is required to work towards implementation of a written "permanency plan" for every foster child.

Permanency planning sometimes represents little more than words on a caseworker's report, however. Mom and Dad often remain unrehabilitated (in fact, they may have disappeared), and Grandma and Auntie often want neither to adopt nor file for legal custody or guardianship and lose the kinship payments. And the consequences of slow or otherwise inadequate permanency planning can be profound. Imagine the young child who spends three, four, five, or more years in the same home, knowing no other parent but the foster parent, but with no assurance that this person, whether a relative or not, will nurture the child to maturity.

Every Family Court judge has handled these heartrending cases of extended foster care. I presided over one just three months into the job. Andy was nearly five years old and had been in foster care for more than four years. Dad never surfaced. Mom was found to have neglected Andy as a result of her drug addiction. She tried rehab; it didn't take. For nearly two years she disappeared, but the foster care agency did not file to terminate her parental rights. Andy's foster care placement was extended three times for twelve-month periods; the judges at those hearings did not force the permanency planning issue. After I inherited the case, the Child Welfare Agency requested a fourth one-year extension of foster care. At the same time, Andy's aunt (his mother's sister) was suing Andy's mother and the commissioner of Social Services for custody of Andy. Mom had resurfaced, in state prison, doing two-to-four years on narcotics charges. She was eligible for parole in a year or so.

Mom, of course, wanted her sister to have legal custody of Andy; she didn't want someone she didn't know raising her son, she said. Moreover, the aunt was caring for Mom's twin boys, Andy's half siblings, whom Mom had voluntarily placed into foster care.

The aunt, it turned out, was a good caretaker.

I ordered visitation between Andy and his half brothers at the aunt's Bronx apartment. The visits didn't go well. The boys were strangers to Andy. He couldn't seem to adjust to them and hated leaving his foster mother. I modified the visitation order so that the visits took place at the home of Andy's foster parent in Brooklyn. But Auntie balked at the trip to Brooklyn and couldn't get along with the foster mother. Andy didn't like his brothers any better in his own house. Andy had suffered from asthma for several years; the visits seemed to bring on attacks.

"The agency's plan is now to reunite the child with his mother once she is out of prison," the OLA lawyer told me at a hearing. "She is very interested in having all three of her children under her own roof again, is undergoing drug rehabilitation in prison, inquires regularly into the well-being of the children, and is trying to arrange visitation at the prison. In the meantime, we think Andy should be moved to his aunt's house so as to encourage the development of his relationship with his siblings and his biological family. At this time, however, we believe it is in the best interests of the child that this be accomplished by continued placement of the child in foster care with the agency, with the aunt as the new foster parent, as opposed to granting the aunt outright legal custody."

"In other words, Mr. Green," I replied, "Andy will have to adjust to two moves, not one, if and when his mother is out of prison. The aunt is just a holding action, right?"

"Well, we can't be certain when the mother is actually going to leave prison, Your Honor," Mr. Green said.

"Why take him away from someone who has been taking excellent care of him and who he has come to know as his only real parent?"

My tone was sharp; the lawyers and the caseworker exchanged glances. I knew what they were thinking: Oh, well, another judge freaks out.

I extended the foster care placement, leaving Andy with his current foster mother, appointed a lawyer for her, and urged her to consider filing for legal custody of Andy. I ordered a once-monthly, two-hour visitation between Andy and the twins to take place at the Child Welfare Agency office in Manhattan under the caseworker's supervision.

Certainly, the authority existed to force the permanency planning issue from the bench. At the end of each twelve-month foster care period, when the Child Welfare Agency applies to extend foster care for another year, Family Court judges can direct the agency to file a case to terminate the parent's rights and thereby seek to free the child for adoption—unless, of course, the agency can demonstrate that it is in the best interests of the child to return to the parent with a specific and realistic casework services plan. From the start, I took a highly activist role in reviewing the reports that foster care agencies are required to file after I place a child in foster care. I recalendared cases if a report indicated to me that services were inadequate or if I believed a case should be filed to free the children for adoption. This approach was time-consuming and turned out to have difficult consequences in terms of getting through the day. I was handling plenty of cases even without these on-the-record jawboning sessions with the caseworkers.

"Your Honor, we'll be filing the termination shortly. The case has been referred to the legal department."

"How long do you anticipate it will take the legal department to file the petition?"

"I don't know, Your Honor."

"Well, how long is it ordinarily, in your experience?"

"It could be anywhere from six months to a year, Your Honor."

"Well, I'm directing the commissioner of social services to file it within ninety days."

"Yes, Your Honor."

So do I calendar the case in ninety days? Do I rely on the child's law guardian to follow up? Do I ask for another written report? As with most Family Court judges, my court calendar was always booked for at least eight weeks. How could I possibly fit in another case?

But I plugged on. Over time, I became increasingly aggressive with the caseworkers. To an extent I sympathized with them. Their pay was low; they had to serve too many families at once. A caseworker with too many active cases is able to concentrate on little more than emergencies. The societal values that these working conditions reflected made me angry. Nevertheless, in the courtroom I would not accept overwork as an excuse for poor casework. Each week, I calendared cases in which a report was overdue or a caseworker had missed a court date. A colloquy of the following kind would ensue:

COURT OFFICER: Your Honor, calling number 32 on the calendar, in the matter of Franco. [To caseworker]: State your name and affiliation for the record.

CASEWORKER: Alice Sloan, Supervisor Two [civil service level].

THE COURT: Ms. Sloan, I had ordered a Child Welfare Agency investigation and report in this custody case on October 20 and adjourned the case for a hearing on October 27, and then on October 27 adjourned it again for a report on November 19. On November 19 the parties and the law guardian were in court on this case, but there was no caseworker or report, so I reordered it and adjourned again until yesterday, November 23. Again yesterday there was no caseworker or report. What's happening?

MS. SLOAN: Your Honor, unfortunately, the caseworker didn't tell me about this case, so I—

THE COURT: Well, at any rate, it appears as though you are telling me the caseworker simply hasn't done the investigation, is that right?

MS. SLOAN: This caseworker has sixty-five cases, Your Honor, and—

THE COURT: Let me interrupt. If you are saying the worker is too busy, I want you to know that is not an acceptable excuse. Five weeks is simply too long for completing an investigation in a case where I deliberately set short adjourned dates for a report.

MS. SLOAN: If Your Honor would set an adjourned date, I will—

THE COURT: When was the last time you spoke to your case-worker about this?

MS. SLOAN: At 9 A.M. this morning.

THE COURT: Well, I appreciate your coming in here this morning on short notice. I'm setting the matter down for hearing tomor-row. Please have the caseworker here with a report on the safety and well-being of these children.

MS. SLOAN: Yes, Your Honor.

THE COURT: Thank you.

MS. SLOAN: Thank you, Your Honor.

I happened to respect this supervisor. I knew she understood that the pointedness of my comments on the public record might help to make her job easier, by increasing the pressure on the caseworker to upgrade job performance in this case.

The key to assuring the well-being of neglected and abused children in any case, as well as the success of family preservation policies, lay in the quality of the Child Welfare Agency's child protective services. So I kept after the caseworkers: Was a parenting skills course necessary? If so, when would the parents be enrolled? If they were already enrolled, were they participat-ing? What measure of achievement was being demonstrated in the program? Was the parent willing to enter recovery for drug addiction or alcoholism? What referrals were being made? What information was available on the specifics of their particular drug program? How successful was the ongoing rehabilitation? Were random drug tests being taken? Where? How often? What were the results? Was psychotherapy or other counseling indicated for the parents or children? Focusing on what? Who would provide it? How often? What were the specific changes being noted as a result? Did the child have special medical needs? How were they being attended to? Were homemaker services required to support the parents? Was a referral for upgraded housing indicated? How long was the waiting list? Was emergency funding available for cribs, clothes, or other necessary items? How long would it take to process the funding? And on and on, every day, in thousands of cases.

Sometimes I would complain to other judges about wanting to strangle some of the caseworkers. The best of these judges would tell me, "Don't get cynical. Don't get into an antiagency syndrome, you'll burn out. There are plenty of good caseworkers and a lot of success stories. Try to keep your balance." And they were right. Competent, conscientious caseworkers with solid supervisors appeared before me every day.

The New York City Child Welfare Agency no longer exists. In its place, Mayor Rudolph Giuliani has created the Administration for Children's Services, the commissioner of which now reports directly to the mayor. Many other changes in the child protective agency's operation are also in the works, including a program to accelerate adoptions and a major overhaul in the way child protective case services are organized. New York State's chief judge, Judith Kaye, has made Family Court the centerpiece of her program to promote the way the courts serve the public. Governor George Pataki's Commission on Child Abuse has recommended a variety of legislative and other changes aimed at protecting children, and state and local legislative leaders are conducting their own hearings and considering reforms. The issues under consideration are vital and broad in scope.

For the Family Court judge, though, the focus remains, day after day, hour after hour, on the case before the bench. In each case to protect children, to assure due process, to remain neutral until the facts are established, to apply common sense and sound judgment within the framework of the law in making decisions—the Family Court judge's charge lies quite outside the arena of public policy, comment, and debate.

One finds one's way. Every judge is alone in the courtroom.

At any rate, with today's sex abuse case over, I ask Bob, "Anything else we can do before lunch?"

"I don't think so."

"Nice case, Judge," Angela says, shaking her head. "That poor kid."

"Perfect way to end the morning," the court stenographer says, rolling his eyes. "Yuchh."

I announce to the staff, "Lunch." Back in the robing room, I change into my suit jacket and hang up my robe, deciding I am too tired to bring it to the dry cleaners.

P.M.

Upstairs, I check my mail, which consists of today's *Law Journal* and an envelope from court administration with the latest statistics on my caseload. I call my wife.

"Oh, hold on, Judge, she just got back from a meeting," Laura's secretary tells me.

"Hi," Laura says. She sounds glad to hear from me. "How's your day?"

"Not too bad. How about yourself?"

"Don't ask," she says.

"You sound beat."

"Actually, I had a productive morning. I'm a little tired, that's all."

"Well, hang in there. The day will be over soon and you can see my wonderful face."

"What do you want to do about dinner?"

"I don't care. We could go out. Speaking of tired, I slept about three hours last night."

"God."

"I had four cups of coffee by 10:30. I don't even have the energy to take my robe to the cleaners."

"I'll pick us up some takeout on the way home."

"Excellent."

"I love you."

"I love you too."

I hang up, thinking when things are good at home, everything else in life seems tolerable.

Opening my refrigerator, which I have been neglecting for months to have repaired, I reach in for an apple and a Diet Coke. Even half-warm, they will satisfy for the moment. Unfortunately, the refrigerator is empty. I find myself trying to remember when I ate the apple, but draw a blank. Once upon a time, before I was a judge, I remembered all the little details of life. Among Family Court judges, reports of post-courtroom brain death are commonplace. For many, it's a coma on a couch after dinner and lights out by 9:30. We fall asleep in movie theaters, or for days at a time lack the energy to pick up the dry cleaning or buy toothpaste.

I look at my new caseload stats, feeling heartened. Somehow I've knocked down the caseload to 728 cases from 805.

I go for food. Outside, the day has turned gray. Crossing Sheridan Avenue, I look at the sunless sky. It's all I will see of it today. I buy a muffin, a Diet Coke, and an apple in a bodega, which has passed its lunch hour peak. One other customer, an 18-B lawyer, is paying for coffee at the cash register.

"Hello, Judge," he says to me.

"Hello, Mr. Serutti, how are you?" I say.

He says nothing, assuming, I am certain, that I don't care if he replies. We stand silently while the clerk makes change and hands him his coffee in a bag.

"Take it easy, Judge," the lawyer says, walking away.

"You too," I say to him.

I pay for my lunch and cross back to the courthouse. I decide to use the Family Court entrance, walking past the crowd lined up switchback-style in the lobby for the metal detector screening, instead of going around the corner to the Criminal Court entrance on 161st Street. Inside, as I head towards the Family Court's public elevators, I hear one of the litigants on the line whisper to her companion, "There's the judge." Looking straight ahead, I continue walking, past the lobby's security desk where a court officer says, "Hi, Judge." I nod at her.

On the elevator, I press against the back wall as bodies jam the car. A probation department supervisor catches my eye. After several stops, when the car has emptied a bit, he slides next to me and says, "Judge, I need to talk to you about that kid you put on probation last week. You know, the one who's going to live in Connecticut with his father."

I remember, sort of. But this is not the time or place for the conversation.

"Well, I—"

"I'll stop by the part later." He flashes a crooked grin. "You know, Judge, I really can't figure out what the hell you're doing in that case."

A surge of anger jolts me. What kind of thing is that to say to a judge, not to mention in the middle of a crowded elevator? As I am about to reply, the elevator opens at the sixth floor and he gets out. "Catch you later, Judge," he says, and breezes away. I take a breath, but my mind is racing. Back in chambers, I try to remember more details about the case and wonder where he got his nerve. I start eating the bran muffin without tasting it.

There's a knock on my door. It's Elaine, here to talk about our case.

Recently, I was presiding in the intake part when Elaine asked me to take a break and discuss something with her in the robing room.

"There's a really unusual case out in the waiting area," she said. "I mean, really unusual."

In the robing room, Elaine tells me that a so-called surrogate mother was seeking to have a sperm donor declared the legal father of a child she expected within the next two weeks. After delivery, and if I ruled that the sperm donor was the legal dad, Surrogate Mom was planning to surrender her parental rights, at which point Dad and his wife, who were Canadians, would be flying home. In Canada, the wife would petition to adopt the child. In the surrogate parenting agreement into which the surrogate mom, the sperm donor, and the sperm donor's wife had entered, the surrogate mom agreed neither to seek legal custody of the child nor to contest any subsequent adoption by the sperm donor's wife.

The surrogate mom was being paid $10,000 for her troubles, as well as all necessary medical expenses. The surrogate mom was also married. The testimony of her husband would also be necessary, in order to overcome the law's presumption that a husband is the father of a child born to his wife.

In the court's waiting area were the surrogate mom, the surrogate mom's husband, the sperm donor, the sperm donor's wife, and a lawyer who wanted the hearing done right away. While it was clear that the lawyer had been retained by the sperm donor and his wife, it was equally clear that the surrogate mom and her husband also considered him to be representing their interests.

"I've never heard of any New York paternity case like this," Elaine starts, "especially where the surrogate mother files. You'd think that the sperm donor would file the case, since he's the one saying he's the father. I'm not even sure it matters. I've got to research it. I think there are a couple of adoption cases, one was in Nassau County, based on surrogacy contracts, but I don't know of any related New York paternity cases."

"So, is any of this kosher?"

"New York hasn't passed any laws regulating surrogate parenting contracts. They've been fighting about it in the legislature for years. I really need to do some research."

"And today?"

"This lawyer wants you to take at least some testimony today, even if you don't finish the case this afternoon. He says the sperm donor and his wife have plane tickets for Canada next Wednesday, so he'd like to complete the hearing before then."

"The kid hasn't even been born."

"It doesn't matter, unless you decide you want blood tests as evidence of paternity. They'd go a little nuts if you did that, it would take a while. If you don't want the tests, you can just take the testimony, declare the sperm donor to be the father, and send them on their way. They're all consenting."

"What do you think?"

"I wouldn't take any testimony today. Just tell the lawyer you're doing intake, you don't do hearings in intake. Once you take testimony, you've accepted jurisdiction. I'd suggest putting the case off until early next week so I can do some research. You might want to think about the public policy issues involved, you know, exchanging cash for babies. There's caselaw on adoptions that might be analogous to this. I want to think about the paternity statute, too, and look at the caselaw. What are paternity cases for? What issues are legitimate for a court to raise besides the issue of who's the father?"

To the group's chagrin, I postponed the case, cutting off abruptly the lawyer's speech about the legitimacy of nontraditional parenting arrangements.

There followed a week of legal research (done mostly by Elaine) and discussions between the two of us. There was no legal precedent. Two adoption cases involving surrogate parenting contracts had been decided in opposite fashion by judges in two different counties, one ruling that surrogate parenting contracts violated New York public policy, and the other stating that there was not necessarily any violation. In any event, these were adoptions, not paternity cases, and decisions by trial court judges had no binding legal effect on me.

Finally, I was ready to draft an opinion. I took the research home, spent the weekend writing, and gave Elaine the draft to review. The lawyer had called her at 9 A.M. today. Surrogate Mom had delivered a seven-pound boy just after midnight. The lawyer wanted to know what was going on.

"What did you tell him?" I asked Elaine.

"That we'd probably have an opinion by the end of the week. Do you want to issue an order forbidding them from transferring physical custody of the baby or leaving New York with him?"

"You think they're going to do that?"

"They might. Mom could get the kid across to Canada, at least. I don't know how much they could get accomplished there. I don't know what Canadian law says about all this. I don't think anybody expected to have trouble with this in New York. I think you surprised them."

"Well, let's get the opinion done. Can you come up to chambers at lunch? I'm not going to issue any orders yet."

"So," I ask Elaine now, "how'd you like the opinion?"

She is sitting on the vinyl couch facing me as I sit in an easy chair across a coffee table from her.

She hesitates, then, "Well, it lays out your position pretty well. It's clear."

"But?"

"Can I be candid?"

"Always."

"Well, it's not solid on the law yet, I don't think. The legal theory isn't clear to me, although I think I know where you're trying to go with the caselaw."

"I get it," I say. "I'm a judge. I'm supposed to rule on the law, not spout philosophy and public policy."

"Well, there is a public policy basis for dismissing the case, but, yeah, you got it."

"See what a genius I am?" I laughed. "I learn so fast."

"Do you want me to fill in some of the blanks?"

"How about all of the blanks?"

"Done. Give me two days."

She leaves. A few days later I would have a good working draft. A week later the opinion was ready. It turned out that what I wanted to do—dismiss the case—had sound basis in New York's Family Court Act and Social Services Law, as well as in several other statutes and rules and in analogous caselaw. Essentially, I ruled that accepting jurisdiction in the case would be improper in view of the strong New York policy, as expressed in the statutes and cases (including a case decided by the Court of Appeals, New York's highest court), prohibiting arrangements involving the exchange of cash or other compensation in matters involving the status of children. I also wrote that New York's paternity statute—Article 5 of the Family Court Act— was written in a carefully considered fashion designed to promote the well-being of children, not just to provide a means to name individuals as legal fathers. The opinion analyzed the caselaw to distinguish legitimate paternity cases from the matter at hand. Case dismissed.

I was careful in the opinion not to rule on whether surrogate parenting itself was legal; it wasn't the issue before me and I didn't need to reach it. "The New York State Legislature has not spoken on this issue; neither is this Court," I wrote, thinking it sounded judicial as hell but kind of pompous. Ten months later, the legislature would make surrogate parenting contracts unenforceable in New York. The issue was ripe for their action. I'm sure my case had nothing to do with the timing.

Elaine called the lawyer and told him the decision, which we faxed to him. To this day I don't know what happened to the kid.

It's nearly 2:30, time to go back to the part. There's a knock at the door.

"Come on in," I yell, then realize the door is locked. I go over and open it. It's Judge Smithson.

"Hi," I say to her at the door.

"Hi. How come you didn't go to the meeting?"

"God. The meeting. I forgot all about it. My mind is gone."
She laughs. "I know what you mean."

Representatives of the New York State Division for Youth,
the agency that supervises the juvenile corrections facilities and
aftercare programs for juvenile delinquents, had met with the
Family Court judges in the supervising judge's chambers at
lunch to describe new programs the agency was implementing.
The meeting had been scheduled for weeks.

"How was your morning?" I ask her.

"Horrible."

"What happened?"

"I don't even want to talk about it. I've got a custody case
that's driving me crazy. I'll tell you about it some time. I want to
go to my chambers. I've got some calls to make before I have to
go downstairs, and I've got to take my kid to the doctor by 6:30."

"OK, see you later," I tell her. As it turns out, I won't see her
again for a week, par for the course in our judicial social life.

Back in the courtroom, Bob greets me with a grin. "You
know who's out in the waiting room? The grandmother from
the writ you issued yesterday in intake. There's a Port Authority
cop with her who wants to be released real bad."

At this news I feel a rush of adrenalin. I'd done a weird one
yesterday in intake and had forgotten about it in the onslaught
of cases afterwards. Now the case was back.

"Is the kid out there?"

"No. They gave the kid back to the mother. They actually
took the grandmother and the kid off the plane at Kennedy."

"They boarded the plane? Sheez." My eyes widen.

"Yeah. You stopped an airplane on the runway, apparently."

"God."

Angela is standing next to Bob, listening. She laughs. "That's real power, Judge."

"Had the plane actually left the gate?"

"I don't know," Bob says. "You want to call the case? We can release the cop."

"Sure. God, I never thought—"

Now I become nervous, not sure just how much detail I want to learn from Grandma. At 3:30 in intake yesterday, on the testimony of a nineteen-year-old mother who had appeared, breathing hard, in my courtroom, I had signed a writ of habeas corpus for the return of her one-year-old baby girl from the young woman's mother, the child's grandmother. As Mom told it, Grandma was about to board a 6:30 flight to Puerto Rico from Kennedy Airport with the baby. Mom and her boyfriend had been living with Grandma until two days ago, when they had moved into the apartment of Grandma's sister (the mother's aunt, the child's great-aunt; in Family Court, figuring relationships becomes as natural as breathing, and as important to survival). The couple was not getting along with Grandma. Grandma agreed to take care of the baby for a few days while they got settled. When they came by yesterday morning to retrieve the baby, Grandma was gone. Checking with relatives and neighbors, Mom learned that Grandma was taking the baby to Puerto Rico. Mom called several airlines, using her mother's name and saying she had reservations to Puerto Rico but had forgotten the flight number.

In the courtroom, she seemed frantic, intelligent, and honest, but you never know. It was either a straightforward baby snatch by Grandma or Mom was running a scam. This was a little more interesting than most of intake, and the clerk, the three court officers, and the half-dozen lawyers waiting their turn in the back of the courtroom had turned their attention to the case.

"Did your mother have legal custody?" I asked her, less for the answer I would get than to assess the mother's demeanor and credibility.

"No, Judge," she answered.

"Is there a welfare case involving the baby?"

"Yes, I'm on public assistance, Judge."

"No, I mean, have there ever been any neglect or abuse charges filed?"

"No, Judge."

"Was this a planned trip to Puerto Rico?"

"No, Judge."

"Why weren't you and your boyfriend getting along with your mother?"

"She's always interfering with the way I take care of the baby, Judge."

"Is your boyfriend the baby's father?"

"Yes, sir."

"Where is he today?"

"He was supposed to meet me here at 3:00. He gets off work at a quarter to three."

Checking the file for cross-references to other court cases involving the family, I see none indicated. I hesitate, looking for flashing red signals in my brain. Then I sign the writ, ordering that the child be returned to the mother, and issue a warrant for Grandma. "Thank you, Judge," the woman says, looking relieved.

And here's Grandma before me now with the uniformed Port Authority cop and a court interpreter. She speaks only Spanish. It must have been some scene on the plane.

"Ma'am, this baby has been returned to your daughter, is that right?"

The interpreter translates, waits for her response, then says, "Yes. I can't believe my daughter did this."

"What do you mean?"

"We'd been talking about going to Puerto Rico for weeks."

"Officer, you're excused. Thank you." The cop leaves. I'd love to have asked a few questions of the cops who boarded the plane, but this was just a transportation officer assigned to bring Grandma to court.

"Well, ma'am, do you have legal custody of this child?" I take a breath and hold it.

"No."

I let out the air. "Has the Child Welfare Agency ever come to your home because the baby was being neglected or abused?"

The translator does her thing and the woman immediately looks confused. My question was too technical. Without waiting for Grandma's response, I say, "Did your daughter take good care of the baby?"

"Yes."

"Well, then, what were you doing taking the baby out of the country without the mother's permission?"

Grandma shrugs. "I don't know."

The picture has become clear. Grandma wasn't baby-snatching, but her behavior wasn't right, either. Did Grandma know that? I couldn't tell and was no longer that interested. She had spent the night in custody; I had overreacted. The writ itself would have assured the baby's return to Mom. Having Grandma arrested had been unnecessary.

Now for the fun part. "Had the plane already left the gate when the police came, ma'am? I mean, had the plane actually started to move?"

"No. It was just about to."

Good stuff. Human drama. But I felt bad about the arrest.

"You're free to go, ma'am. You don't have to come back."

At the bench afterwards, Angela says to me, "She'll never do that again, Judge."

Elaine had returned to the courtroom and heard the last part of the case. "Amazing, Judge," she says.

I laugh and turn to Bob. "Let's call the PINS. It's a diversion case, right?"

"Right."

"Call it."

The case was brought by a mother against her fourteen-year-old daughter for not going to school, staying out late, and being sexually active, a typical "Person in Need of Supervision" (PINS) case filed to declare a child "habitually disobedient" or "ungovernable." The most productive but, sadly, atypical PINS case results in a child's adjustment to a group home and, perhaps, several years in an effective placement facility. Many PINS cases are "diverted"—given a ninety-day cooling-off period, with counseling services under the auspices of the New York City Probation Department—with the agreement of the mother, the child, and the child's law guardian.

PINS cases are controversial. In the first place, many cases conclude with little if any change in the child's life, a source of great frustration for all involved. Not infrequently, the parent (usually the child's mother) drops the case. In other cases, an unsatisfactory situation continues in the child's home. In still others, the parent voluntarily places the child in foster care, an action the parent could have taken instead of filing the PINS case at all.

Moreover, New York law does not permit PINS children to be detained or placed in secure facilities. Thus, although a judge has the authority to issue an arrest warrant for a child who absconds from a group home or other nonsecure facility during a PINS case, for practical purposes the success of a PINS case depends on the willingness of the child to cooperate. That willingness may not be evident; isn't the case in court because the child was alleged to be uncooperative?

The ninety-day diversion period was over in the case before me this afternoon. Noboby has asked me to take further action; case dismissed.

Now lawyers start showing up in droves. This post-lunch phenomenon is common for me and other judges who do not conduct formal calendar calls in the morning. Lawyers respond first to the judges who demand their appearance early in the day, then cover the rest of their cases later in the morning and following lunch.

While I wait for the right combinations of lawyers to appear, I ask Bob to call the third two-sider V case, the one I hadn't asked Elaine to conference earlier. As the parties enter the courtroom, I scan the probation department report I had ordered seven weeks ago when the case was in intake. I check the case papers to determine if Mom and Dad are married. They're not, but Dad was declared the legal father several months ago when Mom brought him to court for child support. It's the standard support—paternity—visitation sequence.

Mom wants support; Dad must be declared the legal father first; then Dad figures he might as well obtain a court order for visitation rights.

The only hitch is the probation report says that Mom claims Dad is a heavy drinker. Mom doesn't want the children, a three-year-old boy and a two-year-old girl, anywhere near him. At least not alone.

"If he wants, he can visit at my mother's house, Judge. She'll watch him while he visits, as long as he doesn't come over while he's drinking."

I look at Dad. He's casually dressed, hasn't shaved, and looks only marginally alert.

"Sir, do you have a drinking problem?" I ask, staring at his face.

"No."

"Well, this woman says you do."

"That's not true."

He can't seem to look at me.

"Ma'am, he says you're making this up."

She laughs and rolls her eyes. "Oh, please, Judge, he barely had a sober day the whole time we lived together."

I make my decision, turning to the man.

"Sir, I believe this woman's statement. I think you have a drinking problem."

He says nothing.

"Well, sir, in some cases I would let a person in your situation visit at the grandmother's house and she would have an order of protection so that if you were drinking or caused a scene, she could call the police. But I'm not going to do that with you. You need to get help and stop drinking first."

I'm trying to get a reaction from him, even an angry denial. Instead, he turns sarcastic. "That's fine, Judge."

"Well, it's really not, sir. It's sad. I'm going to ask you to wait outside the courtroom for someone from the probation department to talk with you about an alcohol treatment program."

He shrugs.

"There's no sense waiting, you ought to go into detox tonight. In the meantime, no visitation with the children. I want the two of you back in court in two months and I'll get an update from the probation department on what's happening with your treatment, sir. Then we can see about supervised visits."

I pick the adjourned date, they leave, and I knock out three quick neglect cases. The first one is another inquest. The next two are scheduled for final disposition, but on the first of these the caseworker doesn't appear.

"Ms. Steinman, do you know where the caseworker is today?" I ask, addressing the OLA lawyer. "He was present at the fact finding six weeks ago and should be aware of today's date."

"Your Honor, he was supposed to be here. I tried to reach his office at lunch, but he wasn't there and nobody knew where he was."

I look at the 18-B lawyer representing the mother. "Mr. McBride, where is your client today?"

"She was here this morning, Judge. She didn't come back from lunch."

"Well, we'll have to adjourn it. Ms. Steinman, please contact your caseworker. As you know, some of my understandably frustrated colleagues are issuing arrest warrants for such caseworkers, and it's more and more seeming like a good idea to me."

"I understand completely, Your Honor," OLA says. They know us like well-worn books, these day-to-day courthouse lawyers. The best of them know exactly what to say to each judge, exactly when to say it, and in what tone besides. You had to admire the way they played us.

The third neglect case involves a final release of three children, ages nine, six, and four, to a mother who seems to have beaten her drug addiction. The children have been living with the mother for the last four months. All random drug tests have been negative during the last year. I obtain the law guardian's consent to the children's release and wish the mother good luck.

"Thank you, Your Honor," Mom says, looking bright-eyed and happy to have ended the case reunited with her children. A success story.

Maybe.

"Judge, there's a violation on an O out there from Part 1," Bob says to me now.

"Uh, what's wrong with Part 1?"

"It's down today. You're coverage."

So I am. I had forgotten that Judge Kerner had the day off.

"Bring it in."

I have a moment of self-pity. Why me? I've got my own calendar to do.

Into the part come a young woman and a big, unshaven, shaggy-haired man who looks as though he hasn't bathed for a week. The case is called while I read the violation papers. From them I learn that the man is the woman's ex-boyfriend, the father of their three-year-old daughter. She has a six-month-old order of protection from Part 1. Last night (according to the papers the woman filed), he came over to her apartment, banging on her door and causing a commotion in the hallway, then punched her when she opened the door. She'd called the police, who arrested him.

I let the police officer who had arrested him leave. Turning to the respondent, I say, "Sir, do you understand what's happening here today?"

"Yes, I think so," the man says.

"Ms. Rollins has accused you of violating the order of protection that was issued in this case. You have the right to have a lawyer to help you with this and if you qualify one can be appointed for you free of charge. Or you can hire your own lawyer. If you are found to have violated the order, you could be jailed for up to six months. It's serious business."

"I want my lawyer in here."

"Fine. I'm going to put this case over until tomorrow, when your lawyer is here and when the judge who issued the order of protection can hear the case. Do you understand?"

"Yes."

"Ma'am, do you understand what is going on here?"

"Yes. Judge, is he going to be in jail until tomorrow?"

"Yes, ma'am, unless he makes bail. The respondent is remanded to the New York City commissioner of correction. One thousand dollars cash bail. The matter will be heard in Part 1 tomorrow."

Bob and a court officer sent up to the part to assist with security for the case put handcuffs on the guy and take him to detention. His face is impassive; he looks hungover. The woman leaves. After Bob returns, Angela comes from the waiting area.

"Judge, the woman wants to drop the violation. She wants to come back in the courtroom."

"What?"

"She told me on the way out. She doesn't want him to spend any more time in jail."

"Well, tell her he's already in. I'm not recalling the case. Why did she bother to file the violation in the first place?"

Bob and Angela look at each other.

"You sure, Judge?" Bob asks.

I try to calm myself. The hell with the guy. Another night in jail won't hurt. Maybe it will teach him not to violate the court order.

Then I remind myself that nobody's proved he violated the order. They are just allegations.

"OK, OK," I say, trying for a humorous tone. "Recall it. I'll hear what she has to say."

Angela gets the woman from the waiting area. Bob retrieves the guy from the detention cell.

"Recalling number 43 on the Part 15 calendar, Your Honor," Angela says, "in the matter of Rollins."

"Now, Ms. Rollins, I understand you have informed the court officer that you wish to withdraw this violation. Is that right?"

"Yes, Judge."

"Why do you want to do that all of a sudden, ma'am?"

"He's spent enough time in jail. I think he has learned his lesson."

"The jail issue is separate from whether you want to charge him with this violation, ma'am. After the violation hearing, he may not end up going to jail, I don't know."

"I don't want to come back any more."

"Well, it's your call, ma'am. Nobody can make you come back. But I'm not letting you drop the case. I'm having a lawyer appointed for you and you can decide after the consultation. The case will be heard tomorrow in Part 1 and he stays in jail overnight."

"Please step out, ma'am," Angela says. The ex-boyfriend is taken away.

A lawyer approaching the table for the next case looks at me as she walks up. "I don't understand these women, Judge. If my boyfriend ever laid a hand on me, I'd have him locked up forever. I'm surprised more of these women don't end up dead."

I say nothing.

The next case is called, a juvenile delinquency case in which a fifteen-year-old is charged with violating the terms of his probationary period. His weary-looking mother stands in the courtroom with him. Eight months ago, her son had been placed on probation after a robbery near the turnstiles of a Bronx subway station. Moving close behind the victim, he had blocked any escape while his partner approached and demanded money. Instead, the brave, or crazy, citizen took a wild swing and shouted for the cops. The kid standing before me and his partner were caught running up the subway station stairs.

The liaison worker from the probation department says to me, "Your Honor, the probation department asked that this case be added to the court calendar upon a filing of a violation of probation against this respondent. Regular attendance at school was a condition of his probation, Your Honor, and he hasn't attended for the last two months. If Your Honor cannot hear the evidence and decide this violation today, the probation department recommends that the respondent be remanded to secure detention pending a hearing."

"Ms. Incantalupo?" I say to the Legal Aid lawyer representing the juvenile.

"Your Honor, at this time on behalf of my client I enter a denial of these allegations and request a hearing. My client came to court voluntarily today at the request of the probation department. He is here with his mother, who is willing to take him home, and I request that he be released to her pending the hearing on the violation."

"Do you have anything to add, Mr. Breen?" I ask the corporation counsel prosecuting the case.

"No, Your Honor, except to say that we concur with the recommendation of the probation department to remand the respondent to CJJ secure pending hearing."

"CJJ secure" means secure detention in the Spofford Detention Center in the Bronx under the auspices of the New York City commissioner of juvenile justice. Detention can also be nonsecure (the juvenile goes to a group home) or open (the judge leaves to the New York City Department of Juvenile Justice the option to choose secure or nonsecure). New York State law permits such detention if a judge finds either of two conditions: a "serious risk" that the juvenile would commit another crime if released, or a "substantial probability" that, if released, the juvenile would not return to court on the next court date.

On the bench, I ask myself whether I should lock this kid up for not going to school. Attached to the violation papers are certified New York City Board of Education records; the juvenile's school attendance is atrocious. His life was going down the tubes, that much was clear. What kind of signal would I send to him today? That he can commit violent crimes and thumb his nose at his probation conditions, then walk? I was willing to bet that reports in the case file showed he had a third- or fourth-grade reading level, if that. Wasn't it time to get serious? Then I tell myself to stop. Being a judge isn't about sending messages. A judge applies the facts to the law. And that's all I need to do to decide this case.

I catch Bob's eye. I barely need to give any facial expression or body language to tell him the kid's going in. I set a hearing date one week away, then say, "The respondent previously committed a violent, predatory act of juvenile delinquency. The probation department has brought forward uncontroverted documentary evidence of his failure to attend school. Thus, pending the hearing, the respondent is remanded to CJJ secure."

"Your Honor, I request that the remand be to nonsecure," the defense lawyer says.

"That application is denied."

"Then at least open, Your Honor."

"No, Ms. Incantalupo."

"Note my exception to the remand, Judge."

Mom watches her son get handcuffed as she leaves the courtroom. She doesn't seem moved, but I am thinking she must be feeling awful. This was once her little baby, after all.

The case moves out and seven other people start taking their places at the counsel table. As the next case readies itself, I find myself thinking of another kid in handcuffs, a twelve-year-old I had arraigned yesterday in intake. While the court officers were bringing him into the courtroom, I was glancing at the case papers. I looked up and felt a shiver. Before me stood a cherub, four feet eight, with moon face and cow eyes. He looked eight, not twelve. His mother was watching me warily, her little dumpling at her side.

He'd put a gun in a citizen's face during a robbery attempt, then pulled the trigger.

Or so the prosecution said.

The gun had misfired.

The defense lawyer had argued for the kid's release home. "Judge, the charges here are only allegations. We deny them. Nothing's been proved. My client has a completely clean record. No truancy, good grades in school, good behavior at home, no prior court involvement, and his mother's here to take him home. The Family Court Act doesn't permit the court to detain a juvenile simply because the state alleges he committed a crime."

I looked at the prosecutor. "Was the gun found?"

"Yes, Your Honor."

"Where?"

"In the respondent's apartment. And there's a confession."

To the defense lawyer I said, "Do you wish to respond?"

"Yes, Judge. There are substantial issues related to the legality of the search and the confession, which we submit was coerced. I object to—"

I cut the lawyer off. "Issues related to the legality of the search and statement are not relevant to the issue of whether to detain the respondent today. In my opinion, there's a serious risk your client will commit another delinquent act if he is released. He's remanded to CJJ secure. Let's set a date for a probable cause hearing."

"Judge, I strongly object. This is a kid with a completely clean record who denies these allegations. There are no grounds to lock him up."

"Your objection is noted."

And off to detention his client went. Some time later I learned the case was dismissed. The search and confession were illegally obtained, one of my colleagues ruled.

The people at the table now are there for a neglect case that is supposed to begin trial. Angela shows the respondents (mother and stepfather) where to stand; their 18-B lawyers stand with them. The Legal Aid law guardian is at one end of the table. Directly across the table from Legal Aid is the city's OLA lawyer representing the Child Welfare Agency. A woman who identifies herself as a social worker stands at the OLA lawyer's left. I begin writing all of these appearances on my endorsement sheet. As Angela calls the case—numbers 1 through 4 on the Part 15 calendar—I am wondering where the caseworker is.

Things quickly become unpleasant.

"This matter is on for fact finding. Mr. Litscomb [the OLA lawyer], are you ready to proceed?"

"No, Your Honor, I'm requesting an adjournment."

"May I ask why?"

"I don't have the medical records, Your Honor. I subpoenaed them but they didn't come."

I glance at the allegations, which consist of a series of beatings of the children by the stepfather in which Mom supposedly acquiesced.

"Well, nevertheless," I say, "why don't we proceed with the caseworker's testimony as to the alleged out-of-court statements to him by the children regarding the beatings? This is a six-month-old case that has already been adjourned three times. Let's get it started."

The OLA lawyer shifts in place. "Uh, Judge, I don't have the caseworker here."

"You don't." Anger starts kicking in, the sarcasm in my voice is a sure sign. Beneath the anger is a feeling of powerlessness, the fear of a situation fundamentally out of my control—and, yes, the fear of looking weak. "Why is that, Mr. Litscomb?"

"Well, Judge, he was here after lunch, but since I had no medical records I assumed the case would be adjourned, so I excused him."

"You excused a witness to this six-month-old child protective proceeding that has never been ready for trial. Isn't that a bit presumptuous? Isn't it the court's decision whether or not a case will be adjourned and for what reason?"

My tone is stern and I am bearing down hard, even though it's pointless. There's no way to proceed with the case and I'm certainly not going to dismiss it. The adjournment has to be granted. But damn it, who runs this courtroom, anyway?

Not I, said the cat.

Immediately, the two 18-B lawyers make passionate arguments for dismissal of the case for failure to prosecute and because due process of law is not being applied to their wrongly accused clients.

I deny their dismissal motions and pick an adjournment date, muttering and sputtering and shaking my head.

Then the OLA lawyer says, "That's not a good date for me, Judge."

"What's the problem, Counselor?"

"It's a Tuesday. That's my intake day, Your Honor."

I move the trial to the next day, a Wednesday, and one of the 18-B lawyers says, "I'm not available that day, Judge. I'm sorry." At least he has the grace to act chagrined.

"Well, why don't the four of you pick a date with the clerk. The court is available to you any Monday through Friday. This matter is adjourned for today. I'm marking the next date final. Be ready to proceed on that date, Mr. Lipscomb."

"Yes, Your Honor."

Marking a child protective case "final" is a pathetic charade. A judge can't simply dismiss child protective cases for failure to prosecute. Child protection comes first.

I grab the rest of my Diet Coke and go into the robing room, trying to calm down and feeling I've made an idiot of myself. Then I realize it was mild stuff, really. Bob walks in.

"Excuse me, Judge. Mr. Paltz from probation wants to know if he can see you for a minute."

My friend from the elevator, still upset about my ruling on the respondent going to live in Connecticut.

I sigh. "Yeah, OK, tell him to come in."

The moment he appears in the door of the robing room, my lunch hour irritation returns. He starts with "Judge, about that—"

"Hold on, Mr. Paltz. I have no intention of discussing this case with you. I made an order, please carry it out."

"But the law doesn't permit—"

"Mr. Paltz, I don't think you heard me. Just do what my order says. If you feel I'm wrong and that you have legal remedies to the contrary, take whatever action you want, that's entirely your choice."

Mr. Paltz's face goes cold, then he leaves. Bob comes back in the robing room.

"He didn't look like a happy camper, Judge."

"I'll bet. Well, anyway, do we have anything?"

"I think I've got everyone together on the next one. Whenever you're ready."

"I'll be right out."

As I stand to walk into the courtroom, Elaine appears at the robing room door.

"Do you have a minute, Judge?"

"What's up?"

"I want to talk to you about a subpoena one of the 18-B lawyers gave me for you to sign. I think there may be some issues with it. You know, you've got a courtroom full of people out there."

"I know. It's a continued hearing on a neglect, with a custody case tracking it."

"I hope you have a scorecard for the players."

"I made good notes last time. Will the subpoena thing be fast? We could wait until five o'clock."

"If you want. I don't think it will take very long."

"Well, I don't feel like going out there, anyway."

A bad sign, talking like that. I'm getting tired.

Elaine puts a subpoena duces tecum on the desk. This is an order for certain case-related documents to be produced in court on a particular date. Here, the lawyer for a mother (it's a neglect case) wants records from a hospital that had treated his client.

"What are the issues you're talking about?" I ask Elaine.

"It's a very broad request, really it's a discovery application by means of a subpoena. He's asked for 'any and all' records relating to his client. I know you mostly just sign these. But this lawyer is so lazy. He didn't even make a discovery demand. Or even give the required notice for the subpoena."

Listening to her, I feel annoyed all of a sudden.

"You mean, I should make him follow the law?"

Elaine laughs. "Something like that."

"Well, then we get exactly what we deserve. No point complaining about legal practice if we're not going to hold their feet to the fire."

"So, how do you want to handle it?"

Bob looks into the robing room. "Whenever you're ready, Judge."

"OK," I tell him and start walking towards the courtroom. "Make him serve the notice and let's see what happens. I'm not signing it yet. Let's send at least the beginning of a message."

"OK, Judge," Elaine says. "Good luck with the mob out there. I'm going to Part 13, Barbara will handle the rest."

I walk into the courtroom. Angela intones, "Come to order, all rise," and I hear chairs scrape and people rustling. I look straight ahead, go to the bench and seat myself, then look up.

Eleven people are looking at me. From left to right are: the OLA lawyer; the CWA caseworker; the father of the two young boys who are the subject of the case; the father's girlfriend of eight months; his lawyer; the mother of the children who was found to have neglected them as a result of her drug use; the mother's boyfriend; her lawyer; the father's sister, who is the current caretaker (kinship foster parent) of the children; her lawyer; and the Legal Aid Society's law guardian for the children. The father's sister has sued Mom and Dad for custody of the two children as well. Her case is also pending.

The psychological studies and other evidence I have received so far tell me that Auntie would be the children's best caretaker. The children, who are all under ten, seem to be thriving with the aunt. Dad had a drug history some years ago, but may be rehabilitated. For the past six months, he's had a job as an assistant porter in an apartment building, but he's only recently settling into a relationship with his new girlfriend. The girlfriend has three kids of her own. In the absence of evidence that Dad is an unfit parent, the law would have him prevail, as the natural parent, against custody claims by the welfare agency or the aunt. Moreover, neither the city nor the law guardian is opposing Dad's desire to have the children.

Mom has given up on custody, seeking only visitation. She hates the aunt. Even with Dad's new girlfriend in the house, she wants Dad to have her kids.

It is the aunt's turn to introduce evidence at the trial. Glancing at my watch, I decide I have time for half an hour of testimony.

"The matter is on for continued dispositional hearing. I believe it is your case now, Mr. Cataldo," I say to the aunt's lawyer.

"Your Honor, may I suggest we have a robing room conference," Mr. Cataldo says. "I believe we may have reached an agreement in this matter."

Immediately, I feel uneasy. I just came out of the robing room. I don't want to go back and get bogged down; it seems doubtful the case can be settled.

"Well, why don't counsel approach the bench instead?" I tell them.

At the bench, off the record, the aunt's lawyer says, "My client wants to drop her custody case, Judge. She says the father can have custody."

I look at him. He shrugs. The other four lawyers exchange glances.

"What's happened, Mr. Cataldo?" I ask him. "Why your client's sudden change of heart?"

"I'm not sure, Judge. They're his kids. I guess she feels he's going to get them sooner or later, it might as well be now."

Turning to the law guardian, I say, "What's your position on this, Ms. Goldman?"

"Your Honor, we've said all along that the kids should go back to the father. He's the natural parent."

"I don't mean as a matter of law, Ms. Goldman. I mean is that your view of the children's best interests?"

"There's no finding of neglect with respect to the father, Your Honor. And in any event, the aunt is consenting at this point."

The law guardian has a point, but I don't like the feeling I have.

"As to your client?" I ask the mother's lawyer.

"She consents, Judge. As long as she can have visitation."

"Let's go back on the record," I tell them.

They return to the table and I summarize the bench conference on the record. I'm not happy, but I can't force a relative to pursue a custody fight. I look at the aunt. She seems close to tears.

"Ms. Berris, did you want to say something to the court?" I ask her. "You seem upset."

She swallows hard, then says, "I don't want to keep the kids from their father. They're his kids. He has a right to them."

I wait, hoping for elaboration. She says nothing. I try coaxing. "Well, you certainly deserve a great deal of credit for the care you've given these children, and I can understand how difficult it must be for you to end that relationship."

Silence. Then, after a moment, the aunt says, "Anyway, they're not acting like they used to. Robert's stopped communicating with me the last couple of months. He comes back from his father's and he's just silent. He had a bump on his forehead and a split lip after his last two visits at his father's house and he wouldn't even tell me what happened."

"This is the six-year-old?"

"Yes," the aunt says.

"Did you ask him what happened?"

"Yes."

"What did he say?"

"He wouldn't say anything."

"Did you ask your brother what happened?"

"Yes, but—"

"Your Honor—" the father's lawyer suddenly interjects.

"Hold on a moment, please, Mr. Teel. You'll have your chance." To the aunt, "Please continue, ma'am."

"He said nothing happened."

"Does the law guardian know anything about this?"

"No, Your Honor."

"Now, Mr. Teel," I say to the father's lawyer, "what did your client want to say about this?"

"May I have a moment to consult with him, Judge?"

"You may."

The father, his girlfriend, and the lawyer whisper together. I am thinking that I should have excluded Dad's girlfriend, and the mother's new boyfriend, from the courtroom altogether. Yet, nobody objected to their being here, and Family Court proceedings are for the most part presumptively open to the public, although few come to watch them. I had no basis for excluding these two. At least, though, I could have had them sit in the back of the courtroom.

His conference over, the father's lawyer says, "Your Honor, my client tells me the bump on the child's forehead came from a tussle he had with one of my client's girlfriend's kids. But he has no idea how the lip injury occurred."

"You don't, sir?" I ask Dad.

"No, Judge," he says.

"You didn't notice his lip was hurt at all?"

"No."

I ask the aunt, "Was the lip bleeding when Robert came home, Ms. Berris?"

"There was dried blood."

I fall silent for a moment, then look at everybody. "OK, folks, I'm not accepting the consent agreement here. The dispositional hearing will continue to its conclusion and I'll decide the matter on the merits. We'll pick a date for that. In the meantime, Ms. Berris, are you willing to continue to care for these two children?"

"It would be a privilege, Judge, Your Honor," she says, starting to sniffle.

"I'm going to try to fit this in within the next two weeks. In the meantime, one visit will be permitted for the parents with the children, except that it will be supervised on-site at the Child Welfare Agency. And I would like the children produced for reinterview by the law guardian, whose inquiry should place emphasis on the circumstances involved in recent visits at the father's home, particularly the injuries."

We spend several minutes identifying a realistic date for completion of the hearing, then an exodus to the courtroom door begins while I take a few deep breaths. I've been concentrating hard.

I reach out to the edge of the bench for the probation department report on the next case. Six weeks ago, a fourteen-year-old had admitted to participating in a group robbery of a twelve-year-old near a bus stop after school. He and three others had surrounded the victim, then one of the four (not this respondent) had taken the victim's baseball jacket. It was the respondent's first offense ("no prior court contacts," in the Family Court jargon). The kid lived with his adult sister, Mom having disappeared into the drug world. His school attendance was less than perfect, but better than many. According to the report, he was reading at fifth-grade level. As the report put it, "the respondent denied involvement with drugs or alcohol," though there was no mention of what his sister reported on that issue.

The report is handwritten, not typed. This sometimes happened in detention cases, since the Family Court Act requires that a sentencing hearing must start within ten days after the end of the trial if a juvenile is detained. The probation department, as with every other agency, claimed to be understaffed; most of the probation officers seemed to me to be working pretty hard. In this case, however, submitting a handwritten report seemed inexcusable. I had released this juvenile to his sister following his admission of guilt and provided the probation department with a six-week adjournment. The statute allows fifty days if the juvenile is released pending sentencing.

In fact, the law requires that probation reports, as well as mental health studies that may have been ordered for the sentencing hearing, be provided five days prior to the hearing date. This rarely, if ever, is the case. Ordinarily, the reports are available to me on the morning of the hearing. Not infrequently, the lawyers and I are still reading them just as the case is being called.

As always, I glance first at the report's last page, looking for the bottom line—the probation department's dispositional recommendation. Here, the recommendation is for an unspecified period of probation supervison. The law permits up to two years.

As I read the rest of the report, deciphering the handwriting and looking for helpful information, I notice a lawyer walk into the courtroom and head for the robing room. I had appointed her as law guardian for three children, ages ten, seven, and six, in a custody proceeding. Mom and Dad, neither of whom had lawyers, were on the sixth floor for a hearing on child support issues. They were supposed to appear before me afterwards on the custody issue.

The lawyer peeks into the robing room, asks Barbara if she can speak with her for a moment, then goes in, closing the door behind her. I start wondering what it's about. Meanwhile, the players are entering the courtroom for the delinquency case: the juvenile and his older sister, the corporation counsel and Legal Aid lawyer, and the probation department liaison worker. The case is called and a moment later I begin the script.

"This is the dispositional hearing in the matter of Grayson, which has now commenced. The probation department's investigation and report is made part of the record as court's exhibit A for the purpose of disposition without prejudice to the right of any party to examine the maker of the report."

Then, to the probation officer, "Mr. Chapa, are you familiar with the file in this matter?"

"Yes, Your Honor."

"Is the probation department prepared to make a dispositional recommendation?"

"Yes, Your Honor."

"What is that recommendation?"

"We are recommending that the respondent be placed on probation," he says, reading from his notes.

"And in the opinion of the probation department, is that the least restrictive dispositional alternative at this time consistent with the respondent's needs and best interests and the need for community protection?"

This question tracks the Family Court Act's language containing the legal criteria for a juvenile delinquency sentence.

"Yes, Your Honor."

To the corporation counsel, "Does the presentment agency have anything to add?"

"No, Your Honor. The presentment agency rests and agrees with the recommendation."

To the Legal Aid lawyer, "Mr. Pauli, will the respondent be calling any witnesses or presenting any other evidence?"

"No, Your Honor. We consent to the recommendation of probation."

New York State law structures juvenile delinquency cases so that a judge cannot declare a child a juvenile delinquent, even after the judge finds that the child committed a crime, until there is a further determination that he or she requires supervision, treatment, or confinement. This case was straightforward in that regard. The respondent had committed a serious act involving the terrorizing of a young boy. Yet, this was his first offense, he wasn't the ringleader, his sister seemed willing and able to cooperate with the probation department, and I had no evidence of other negative behavior, such as drug use or truancy. I was required by the Family Court Act to choose the "least restrictive" dispositional alternative at sentencing. The other main juvenile delinquency sentence available, placement in a New York State Division for Youth correctional facility for up to eighteen months, would not be appropriate in this case: I would first have to find that the respondent required "confinement." Balancing the law's requirement to protect the community with the law's requirement to serve the needs and best interests of the child, I did not feel I could properly confine him as the "least restrictive" sentence.

New York State law is clear that the purpose of juvenile delinquency cases is to rehabilitate, not punish. I wasn't a Criminal Court judge. Surely it was possible—wasn't it?—to rehabilitate this juvenile at home and still protect the community.

Assuming, of course, that his sister and teachers and the probation department did their jobs and that the kid was motivated, assumptions I had learned could not be readily made.

So I finish the hearing with the standard language, "The court finds by the required quantum of proof that the respondent requires supervision. He is adjudicated a juvenile delinquent. The court finds that the least restrictive dispositional alternative at this time consistent with the respondent's needs and best interests and the need to protect the community is that the respondent be placed on probation for a period of eighteen months. All of the usual terms of probation will apply, but I want to emphasize in particular"—here I look directly at the kid, catching his eye—"that you must go to school every day unless you have a good excuse not to, Mr. Grayson, and not commit any more crimes. Do you understand?"

The kid is silent for a moment, then says without emotion, "Yes."

No Big Brother chats or Stern Father lectures from this judge. Would thirty seconds of judicial heart-to-heart, however sincere and well-meaning, begin to reverse a dozen or more years of mental or emotional pathology; parental abuse, neglect, or incompetence; educational system failure; and inadequate or ineffective community services? Any or all of these might be contributing in any particular case.

Or, perhaps, it might be something else: bad character. More and more for me, the issue was values. Recently, for example, I had presided over a juvenile delinquency case in which a fourteen-year-old respondent was charged with raping and sodomizing his teenage sister soon after she came from Mexico to live with her mother and two brothers in the Bronx. Finding herself pregnant from the rape, she finally told her mother, who called the police. Only her words, as translated from the Spanish by the official court interpreter, can convey the horror.

(Evidentiary objections and rulings are omitted below.)

PROSECUTION: And when your brother came into the room, what, if anything, did he say?

WITNESS: I was making the bed. He came in and kissed me on the mouth—and I asked him why he did that. He said he—he hadn't meant to do that, that he wanted to kiss me here [the cheek], and to excuse him because he did not want to do that.

PROSECUTION: What did he do after he said that to you?

WITNESS: He grabbed me here [by the wrists].

PROSECUTION: Continue.

WITNESS: He acted as if he was playfully wrestling with me, and he laid me on the bed, and he kept looking at me, and I asked him why he was looking at me that way, and he did not answer. He kept looking at me.

PROSECUTION: What did he do after that?

WITNESS: I was pushing him away, and I was telling him not to do anything to me, and he pulled my pants down and my underwear.

PROSECUTION: And what did he do after he pulled your pants down and your underwear down?

WITNESS: He put his penis in my vagina.

PROSECUTION: When he did that to you at that time, did you feel that you could get away from him?

WITNESS: I was pushing him, but his weight was on me. He had his weight on me here, and he said that even if I said anything nobody would do anything about it.

PROSECUTION: What, if anything, occurred after he held you on the bed?

WITNESS: He made me bleed, and then he got off me, and I went to the bathroom, and I started to cry, and I asked him if he knew how much harm he had done to me.

PROSECUTION: And what, if anything, did he say in response?

WITNESS: He didn't know when—how to tell when a woman had never had sex before.

PROSECUTION: And you indicated you were bleeding. From where were you bleeding?

WITNESS: From the vagina.

PROSECUTION: And how long did that bleeding last?

WITNESS: For a while.

PROSECUTION: After that incident, how did you feel emotionally?

WITNESS: I felt very bad. I had always seen my brother—I always remembered him as he was when he was a little boy, and I did not believe what had happened with him. He was always a little boy that I loved a lot, and it was not fair that he had hurt me this way.

•   •   •

PROSECUTION: So after the January incident, you didn't tell your mother about that?

WITNESS: No.

PROSECUTION: You didn't tell your father about that happening?

WITNESS: No. I told no one. Sometimes my mother would see me cry, and she would ask me what was wrong, and whenever I tried to be alone with her, he [my brother] would get in the way and he would pull me by the hair, and he told me not to talk.

•   •   •

PROSECUTION: And during the incident at the end of February, what did he do?

WITNESS: He forced me to have sex with him again, and I did not want to, but he told me that nothing bad would happen and he threatened me.

PROSECUTION: When you say that he forced you, how did he force you to have sex with him?

WITNESS: He would always grab me here [by the wrists]. I would tell him that I was going to tell my mother, and he told me not to say anything to my mother. He said they would not believe me because I was already older than he was, and that if I said anything it would seem as if I had taken advantage of him.

PROSECUTION: Now when you indicated he had sex with you at the end of February, what specifically did he do?

WITNESS: He put his penis in my vagina.

PROSECUTION: And what, if anything, else did he do?

WITNESS: And also through the anus.

PROSECUTION: And what, if any, injury occurred because of those actions?

WITNESS: He made me bleed through the anus. I screamed and I couldn't take the pain, and he said, okay, that he wouldn't do it through there anymore, and it hurt me, but he said he would continue through the other part and he did so.

The respondent did not testify, as was his right. My findings were of sodomy and rape, which permitted me, at sentencing, to place the juvenile respondent in a New York State Division for Youth facility for three years, with at least one year to be spent in the most secure type of facility.

At the sentencing hearing, the respondent presented six witnesses, including a psychiatrist, a psychologist, a social worker, and a probation officer, as well as a doctor and a research scientist from an outpatient sex offender treatment program associated with a New York hospital. All but one of these witnesses recommended that the respondent be spared secure placement. A private (i.e. non-Division For Youth) non-secure residential program was recommended by one witness. This program permitted the respondent to visit home, where the victim was still living. Several other witnesses suggested that a "limited" secure facility, which also permitted home visits, would be adequate. After all, said four of the six witnesses, the respondent's sexual conduct had been "intrafamilial" and thus did not warrant the same degree of secure placement or type of approach to treatment as when the victim is a stranger. One witness even suggested that an explanation for the rape and sodomy might be found in "the sister's recent arrival in the United States."

Good Lord, I said to myself, holding my tongue and listening to these so-called experts.

The respondent chose not to testify at the sentencing hearing, either. He told the shrinks, and anyone else who would listen, that the sex was consensual, though he conceded that he had since learned, from his fellow detainees at the juvenile detention center, that it was wrong to have sex with one's sister. The psychologist offered a diagnosis of "conduct disorder." The respondent could barely read and had rarely attended school last year. He divided his time between his mother's home in the Bronx and his father's home in Brooklyn. Both households were, as the expression goes, dysfunctional; the probation reports yielded evidence of child neglect. I ordered the Child Welfare Agency to perform its own investigation.

Then the respondent produced nine letters written to him by the victim since the trial. These private communications, which she had sent to the respondent at the detention center, were offered to imply that the sex had in fact been consensual, although nothing she wrote suggested that. The argument was that a victim of rape and sodomy would not maintain contact with her abuser. I read the letters. They were sad evidence of a disturbed young woman who still loved her younger brother despite his brutality. They added nothing to the dispositional hearing; they informed me about her, not the respondent. I declined to admit the letters into evidence. They were irrelevant.

I could not change this violent respondent's past: the poor upbringing and lack of education. But I could address his future. In my opinion, his best interests and the need for community protection could only be served in the most secure setting. First of all, the victim would be safe from him while she began to heal. Second, the respondent would be a captive audience for the formal education he so badly needed and had shown he would not obtain outside. The rest of the respondent's rehabilitation, in my opinion, needed to be grounded in a view of him as suffering from character defects. Here, I believed, was no subject for a study of sociopathic evil; the respondent was, at bottom, merely lazy, dishonest, and lustful for power over people.

How could I best promote the likelihood of changing him? First, by showing him that the consequences of his behavior would devastate his life, not just the lives of his victims. Second (if he was unwilling to change), by providing an unmistakable demonstration that his behavior was unacceptable to the rest of us. In short, I had to get his attention.

I gave the respondent the maximum.

That night, the hearing concluded, I described to my wife how I felt as I gave my decision from the bench to an unusually crowded courtroom.

"It was strange. I thought I sounded like a pompous school principal at assembly."

"You were self-conscious," Laura said. "It was an unusual case. A lot of people were watching."

"No, it was something else. I really didn't like the kid."

"Well, my God, look what he did. What would have happened to him in adult court?"

"It would depend on whether he got juvenile offender treatment after the indictment, which he probably would have. I think the maximum would have been three-to-ten, I'm not sure. Unless, of course, a jury decided he didn't do it."

"Did you have any doubts about that?"

"No."

"So?"

We were silent for a moment. Then Laura said, "Let it go, Rick. You did what you thought was right. That's what judges do. Your words."

"I guess so."

"Tomorrow there'll be another sixty cases."

"Count on it," I said.

Now I go back to the robing room, curious about the conversation Barbara is having with the law guardian on the custody case. Opening the door, I see Barbara seated at the desk and the lawyer, an 18-B named O'Neil, standing near one of the chairs along the wall. She seems agitated. Barbara starts getting out of her seat.

"Barbara, sit, it's OK," I tell her, but she stands anyway. "What's going on?" I ask.

Barbara says, "Judge," then the 18-B lawyer, who is supposed to appear before me on the main custody issue, interrupts.

"Judge, the mother and father are downstairs," the lawyer says. "They were still waiting for the hearing examiner when I came up here. They say they have everything settled between them. The father wants to withdraw his custody petition once the support order is entered. They've agreed on a support amount. I don't think you ought to let him withdraw the custody case, or at least you should order a CWA investigation. I think this mother is—"

"Ms. O'Neil, hold on a second. Excuse me, you're going a little fast."

In fact, she is nearly hysterical. Her voice is high-pitched and she has hardly stopped to breathe. "Did you get a chance to see the kids?" I ask her.

"She only brought the little one, Judge. I couldn't get much out of him, but I think there's something going on in that house."

"What?"

"I don't know. The kid seems depressed, or sick, and the mother and father are in some kind of collusion. I really think you should—"

"When are they going to be finished down there? Do we know?" I look at Barbara.

"I'll call," Barbara says. She gets on the phone, then tells me, "They're before the hearing examiner now, Judge. They said about five minutes."

Now Bob appears at the robing room door. "What's happening with this, Judge?"

"That's what we're trying to find out. They're supposed to be upstairs in five or ten minutes."

"You want me to go down and get them?"

"No, I don't think so." I turn to Ms. O'Neil. "Listen, do you think these three kids will keep until tomorrow? I mean, there's no emergency in what you think you're seeing, is there?"

"I wouldn't call it an emergency, Judge. It's just that I think these two shouldn't be allowed to do whatever they want to without—"

I stop her again. A teary film has begun to fill her eyes.

"Please calm down, Ms. O'Neil. Look, I don't want to deal with this case under time pressure. I'll have Barbara tell them to come back tomorrow and to bring the three kids. I'll hear it tomorrow and I'm asking that you put everything that you said in here on the record."

The lawyer looks relieved. "OK, Judge. As long as somebody tells the mother to bring the kids. I really need to talk to them."

"Done," I tell her.

The 18-B lawyer leaves. When she is gone, Bob says, "I thought we were going to have to send her to the clinic."

I laugh. "Well, let's do the last two Os."

Giving the first case a quick once-over on the bench, I discover it contains an allegation, among others, that Dad had fired a gun into the floor of the apartment during a temper tantrum. The bullets had ricocheted around the living room. He and his wife had three young children. In intake, the Part 8 judge ordered Dad removed from the home the day Mom filed the case.

After I advise Dad of his rights, he waives counsel and a hearing, and consents to a final order of protection excluding him from the home. I tell Mom to wait outside the courtroom for a copy of the order of protection.

"Judge," she says, "I do want him to be able to visit with the children."

What's this?

"Sir, where are you living now?" I ask Dad.

"You mean right now?"

"I mean, what is your current address?"

"My current address?"

This is less than smart, messing with the judge late in the afternoon on a gun case. I tell myself that if he wants visitation, he can file a separate case. I don't want to deal with this now.

But something is making me uneasy. I take a breath to summon another few minutes of energy.

"Sir, listen to me. I want to know what your current living address is. Where do you live?"

"At work."

"At work? What's the address of your place of employment?"

He gives it.

"And who do you work for? What's the name of the business or company? I also want the telephone number."

He provides the information and I write it on the endorsement sheet.

"What do you do there?"

"I'm a security guard. They let me stay there overnight in a maintenance room."

"What shift do you work?"

"Eight to four."

I turn to the woman. "Ma'am, where do you propose this child visitation take place? And what makes you think these children are safe with this man? I mean, even though I haven't heard any evidence in this case, you did say on the petition that he once fired a gun in the house."

"That was three years ago, Judge."

"Excuse me?"

"In Germany. We were there when he was in the army. He hasn't done anything like that since. He could visit with the kids at his mother's house. She'd watch out for them."

So, Dad was living with his mother. For some reason, they hadn't wanted me to know.

"A Child Welfare Agency investigation is ordered," I announce for the record. "CWA is to visit the mother's home, the paternal grandmother's home, and the father's place of employment and report on the circumstances and well-being of the children on the adjourned date."

I fix my eyes on the woman. "Ma'am, if you permit any visitation for the children with this man until I have the results of this welfare agency investigation, I am going to order them to take your kids away from you. Do you understand?"

With a blank face she says, "Yes, Judge."

I pick an adjourned date for the case. I don't trust Mom, not to mention trigger-happy Dad.

They file out. The next case comes in. The petitioner is a woman who claims that the respondent—her ex-boyfriend—has been stalking her for several weeks, in violation of an order of protection I had granted her five months ago. New York State's Penal Law includes stalking in the crime of harassment, which is one of the crimes that this woman's protective order covered. Reading her new petition, I learn that she has been seeing her former boyfriend, who lives up the block from her, more and more often on the street, near her building, and in the bodegas.

The guy stands before me, projecting a street poser's attitude of defiance and aggression. When Angela asks him if he swears to tell the truth, so help him God, he shrugs and says, "Why not?"

"Is that a yes, sir?" I ask him.

"I guess so."

"What does that mean?" My voice gets sterner and I stare him down.

He shrugs again. "Yes."

When they are seated, I ask him, "Are you going to want a lawyer in this case?"

"What do you think I should do, Judge?" he asks with casual sarcasm.

"It's entirely up to you, sir. If it is proved to the court that you committed a violation of the order of protection that was issued against you, you could be jailed for up to six months. It's a serious matter."

"What violation?" he says.

"Sir, what is that in your hand?"

"This? The cops gave it to me."

"Have you read it?"

"Not really," he lies.

"Well, take a few minutes right now and read it carefully. I'll wait for you."

He makes a show of reviewing the papers.

"Are you finished, sir?"

"Yeah."

"Do you understand what's going on here this afternoon?"

"I guess so."

"Well, do you want a lawyer?"

"Yeah."

"Are you employed?"

"No."

"How do you support yourself?"

"I had a savings account."

"What do you mean, had?"

"Well, it's gone."

"Then how are you supporting yourself now?"

The woman says, "He works, Judge. He's lying."

I turn to her. "Ma'am, I haven't asked you to say anything. Please don't interrupt."

She is glaring at the guy and Bob moves between them, standing a few steps back from the table out of sight.

"Sir, I asked you how you support yourself."

"My friends help me."

"This woman here says you work. Do you realize that you are under oath?"

He says nothing. I don't want to appoint a lawyer for him; the taxpayers (including me) shouldn't have to pay for this. But he obviously is going to stick with his financial hardship story. Moreover, it will delay the case significantly if I tell him to bring his own lawyer. If he bothers to shows up next court date, he'll no doubt have no lawyer with him. He'll simply tell me the same thing.

I scribble a note and hand it to Ethel, who is sitting to my right. Angela comes over and takes it. The note reads, "He's going in."

"OK, sir. I'm going to appoint a lawyer for you and put the case on for a hearing tomorrow. Ma'am, how do you support yourself?"

"Public assistance."

"I'm appointing a lawyer for you, too, ma'am. You'll come back tomorrow and the violation petition will be heard. You may step out now."

The two of them turn towards the courtroom door.

"Not you, sir," I say, and the court officers move towards him.

"You're spending the night in jail. I'm remanding you to the New York City commissioner of correction. From your demeanor and tone of voice this afternoon I believe you present a substantial risk of not returning to court for the hearing. Bail is set at one thousand dollars cash."

Bob and Angela take him out the courtroom's side door, towards a detention cell. Soon they return.

"Judge, he didn't know what was happening at first," Bob says. "When we explained it and I told him bail was one thousand dollars, he said 'Good, I've got one hundred bucks on me right now. Where do I pay?' I told him it was one thousand dollars cash, not a bond. I'll tell you, he was not pleased."

One more case to go.

Across the courtroom from me, awaiting my decision in a complicated termination of parental rights proceeding, sits a mother of three children, ages eight, five, and three. The children had two different fathers; both had long since slipped into the void. Five years had passed since the oldest child was placed in foster care because of the mother's crack addiction. The middle child and the baby were born positive tox. Mom made two unsuccessful attempts at rehab. During the trial, she made a third try at staying clean, lasting just three months. She then tested positive for cocaine two weeks before the conclusion of the trial and checked herself back into rehab.

Meanwhile, the three children were thriving in the same foster home. The nonkinship foster parents wanted badly to adopt them.

Now, Mom's lawyer pleads for her, "Your Honor, the mother is simply asking for one more chance. A suspended judgment to see whether her recovery from drug addiction can finally take hold. We all know that recovery from this disease may begin in fits and starts, and I ask you to look at her past attempts at rehabilitation not as failures but rather as part of the process of her getting better. She loves these children and believes she can eventually be a good parent for them. We ask you not to break the parent-child bonds forever."

The foster care agency's lawyer replies, "Judge, if there are any bonds that ought not to be broken in this case, it is the strong bonds that have formed between the three children and the foster parents, who are the only real parents these children have known. By our constant referrals to drug programs for the mother and our many attempts to involve her in counseling and therapy, the agency has put forth extremely diligent efforts to reunite this family, as Your Honor decided at trial. If we had not tried so diligently to bring this mother and her children safely together, then we would not have been entitled to this hearing. The caselaw is clear that it is not our responsibility ultimately to succeed with those efforts; it is our job to provide the services, but success is up to the parent. There comes a point where the mother has had sufficient chances and the timing is appropriate for terminating parental rights. Even assuming the mother were now to use a period of suspended judgment to rehabilitate herself, would it be in the best interests of these children at that late date to remove them from their foster home and hope, against all evidence, that the natural mother can properly take care of them—and that the children can recover from the shock of losing the loving care they have received from their preadoptive parents all these years? I think not."

The law guardian for the children echoes the foster care agency's sentiments.

Then I rule, terminating the mother's rights, deciding that it would be an act of cruelty after this much time to end the children's relationship with the foster parents. The three kids deserved better than this unfortunate soul who was their mother. She might recover, but it was the children's best interests, not hers, that constituted the legal issue at this stage of the case.

For a few seconds, Mom puts her head down on the courtroom table and appears to start weeping. Suddenly she looks up at me and says, "You took my kids away, you son of a bitch. You'll pay for this, you motherfucker. Nobody's going to take my kids away from me. You're going to get yours, you—"

"Ma'am, that's enough," Angela says, moving towards her.

I take the case papers into the robing room to get out of her sight and to make endorsements. Such was the downside of ruling from the bench in a sensitive case. But the alternative of reserving decision was too time-consuming in a case without remarkable legal or factual issues.

Not long after that incident, I was knocking out a large but uncomplicated calendar on a fine morning, banging along in sprint mode, when the captain of the Bronx court officer command, his lieutenant, a third officer, and the chief court clerk walked into the courtroom. I took a break.

"A distinguished group," I said to them. "Have I been promoted?"

"Not exactly, Judge," the captain said. "Can we go into the robing room?"

The five of us, in addition to Barbara and Bob, made for a crowded meeting. We stood. The captain said, "We got this."

He handed me a one-page, single-spaced typed letter, unsigned and undated, that began with "Dear Judge Ross, you're dead. You won't make it to Christmas. You'll never know what hit you" and went downhill from there.

Feeling strangely calm, I looked at the captain.

"That's lovely," I said to him. Bob was reading a copy of the letter.

"May I see it, Judge?" Barbara asked. Bob handed the letter to her.

"So what happens now?" I asked.

Perhaps because I didn't want to accept the potential seriousness of the situation, I found myself expecting the group to offer ironic replies, such as "Better enjoy every day while you can," or "Might as well start smoking and drinking," or some other lame joke. Instead, the captain said, "We put you under guard for a while. Whoever wrote this probably has no intention of taking action, but it's better not to assume anything."

Still not ready to get the point, I asked jocularly, "So when do the bodyguards appear on the scene?"

"They already have," the captain replied, pointing at Bob and the officer who had accompanied them into the courtroom.

"Whoa," I said.

"Well, I wouldn't get unduly worried. We get these kinds of threats from time to time but nobody's followed through yet with a Family Court judge."

Suddenly I had a clear thought, "What about my wife?"

"Well, there's no indication from the letter that the writer knows anything about you. Is either of you in the phone book?"

"No. You can't get either of us from information, either."

"Good. We've already called your local precinct. They'll make sure to have a car cruise by now and then. Does your building have a doorman?"

"Yes."

"We'll have the cops speak to them. You don't have to."

I was starting to get it. "So, uh, how does this work?" I asked.

"We'll go a week at a time, starting with a fairly high level of protection, and evaluate the situation as we go along," the captain said, and proceeded to outline the details of the security.

My guards were well trained and highly dedicated. The security was smooth and, to the extent possible, unobtrusive. Wherein lay the rub. "To the extent possible" frequently meant, and necessarily so, a complete lack of privacy. It took about a day and a half for me to work up a fury at the letter writer.

"It's awful," I told Laura on the phone. "They're all over me."

"That's good, right?" she said. "Don't complain. Nobody's guarding me."

"Do you want protection? I think I can get it for you."

"Nah, nothing's going to come of this, you watch. It's just some nut. That's a heck of a job you've got."

"Well, keep your eyes open on the subway," I said.

Adding to the week's excitement—and discomfort—was the presence of a house guest, a relative from out of town who, thank goodness, considered the event little more than a terrific story to tell back home.

"New York is even wilder than everyone says," she exclaimed the first night. "I love it. Can I take the bodyguards home with me?"

Despite her good humor, and the fact that she was a sensitive and interesting companion, I felt an added responsibility until she left, safe, a few days later.

Laura's comment—"That's a heck of a job you've got"— haunted me. Perform any job day after day and you are bound to stop considering, even noticing, its special aspects. The death threat sobered me. And it made still more concrete the wall I sensed forming around me from the moment I took the oath. Much of the remaining bloom came off the judicial rose.

Day after day I plugged along. On days when I felt less than my best, I forced myself to concentrate harder. It was as though the public, and especially the children in the endless stream of cases, represented an audience I was charged with satisfying each day. I began to understand—as, for example, a professional athlete or entertainer would—that the proper measure of job success was not in the occasional sparkling performance or dud. Rather, the goal was to bring forth consistently good quality work: reliable, finely honed basic chops, as though I were a top-flight studio musician.

For today, though, no more cases. I hang up my robe and put on my suit jacket. Back in the courtroom, I review the clerk's annotated calendar, making the daily count. I'd done fifty-seven cases. (Court administration counts each child as a case; a case involving adults but no children also gets a count of one.) The fifty-seven cases represented thirty-five families. For Bronx Family Court, middle-of-the-road volume. More than half of the cases—thirty in all—had reached conclusion. If I obtained final dispositions in one-third of the cases on the calendar each day, that disposition rate, I figured, would keep my caseload in some reasonable degree of manageability. From that standpoint, the day had been quite productive.

Had justice been done? Were the needs and best interests of the children and families of New York City, and the community's need for protection, adequately served?

I wasn't asking. Tomorrow's calendar will be larger, starting at fifty-eight. I sign the remaining orders Ethel has prepared for me, thank the court staff for a good day's work, and leave the courtroom.

I am hoping Laura will be home by the time I get there.